Also by Judith Jones

The Tenth Muse: My Life in Food

WITH EVAN JONES

The Book of *New* New England Cookery
The Book of Bread
Knead It, Punch It, Bake It!

WITH ANGUS CAMERON

The L. L. Bean Game and Fish Cookbook

The Pleasures
of Cooking for One

The Pleasures

of Cooking for One

Judith Jones

Alfred A. Knopf New York 2009

To my great grandchildren,
Jonah and Odessa and Cooper and Shepard.
May they be blessed with the Muse and enjoy the pleasures
of cooking.

This Is a Borzoi Book Published by Alfred A. Knopf

www.aaknopf.com

Knopf, Borzoi Books, and the colophon are registered
trademarks of Random House, Inc.

Portions of this work originally appeared in *O, The Oprah Magazine.*

Library of Congress Cataloging-in-Publication Data
Jones, Judith, [date]
　　The pleasures of cooking for one / Judith Jones.—1st ed.
　　　　p.　cm.
ISBN 978-0-307-27072-6
　　Includes bibliographical references and index.
　　1. Cookery for one.　I.　Title.
　　TX652.J6723　　　2009　　　641.5'61—dc22　　　2009012307

Manufactured in the United States of America
Published October 1, 2009
Second Printing, October 2009

Illustrations credits　　All photographs by Christopher Hirsheimer,
with the exception of the following pages: Chris Vandercook: 73, 123, 205,
and 212; Ken Schneider: 115; Bronwyn Dunne: 128.

Contents

Introduction

After my husband, Evan, died in 1996, I was not sure that I would ever enjoy preparing a meal for myself and eating it alone. But as I described in *The Tenth Muse: My Life in Food,* I was wrong, and I soon realized that the pleasure that we shared together was something to honor. I found myself at the end of the day looking forward to cooking, making recipes that work for one, and then sitting down and savoring a good meal.

A number of readers responded to the section in my book on cooking alone, with its sample recipes. One woman told me that she hadn't cooked in several years, since her husband died, but that my experience encouraged her to get going again, and she wanted more ideas. I was particularly pleased that young people on their own for the first time would approach me asking how to get started, what basics and what equipment they needed. They wanted to make for themselves relatively inexpensive, healthy, and, of course, delicious meals, but most cookbooks were too daunting and did not address the single fledgling cook on a tight food budget. I've also talked to so many live-alones who have been too busy with their careers, but who like good food and have gradually come to feel that they've been missing something.

Fifty-one percent of the population in the New York metropolitan area lives alone. Yet no one seems to cater to their needs. Supermarkets do everything they can to make us buy more than we need, and the food industry has for more than a century been selling the idea that it is demeaning for women to cook and a waste of time when they can buy ready-made products instead. So I felt compelled to write this book to

share with you the strategies I have devised for beating the system. It isn't a cookbook for what Julia Child used to call "the flimsies"—that is, people who aren't genuinely interested in cooking and want fast and easy recipes and shortcuts at the expense of taste. This book is for those of you who want to roll up your sleeves and enjoy, from day to day, one of the great satisfactions of life.

I do, however, hear the naysayers protesting. Yes, I like to cook, they say, but I like to cook for *others*, to give my friends pleasure. Why would I want to go to all that trouble just for me? My answer is: If you like good food, why not honor yourself enough to make a pleasing meal and relish every mouthful? Of course, we want to share with others, too, but we don't always have family and friends around. And I can't see taking in my neighbors every night.

Others object to the expense involved, and the waste. You have to go out shopping, they complain, and buy all those pricey ingredients that chefs call for, and you can't use them up before they turn rotten. Leftovers are boring; who wants to eat cold lamb all week? Actually, it's all a matter of strategy. Moreover, you are in charge of what you're cooking, picking your own ingredients, deciding how much fat or salt or sugar you want to consume and whether you want to spend extra to have grass-fed, local beef or an organic farmyard chicken.

Cooking for yourself is particularly creative because you are inspired by what's in your fridge or freezer or garden or nearby market. You don't have to follow a recipe slavishly; you can substitute as you like—planning how to make three quite different dishes from, say, a tenderloin of pork—putting leftovers to good use, taking advantage of leftovers, having in the freezer certain basic items, and so on. If you follow the tactics I recommend, what you save on food costs will astonish you.

Another advantage to cooking for yourself is that you have only yourself to please. So you can indulge in a sudden whim. You can choose to make just what *you* feel like—perhaps only a light, simple supper dish or a salad if you've consumed a rich meal at lunch that day. There's no need to be a perfectionist, trying to win applause from your guests. If a sauce curdles, you'll eat it anyway. And you'll learn from your mistakes.

I suspect that a lot of Americans eat too much just because it's there on the plate. They've got to clean it up. But if you deliberately set aside several chunks of meat from the stew you've made to use in a bean dish for a second round, you feel good about not gobbling it all up, already anticipating its reincarnation.

Then there are what I call "cook's treats." For instance, that package of giblets that comes with a whole roasting chicken: the liver can be used to make yourself a delicious shirred egg for breakfast or lunch; the giblets and neck will go into a soup pot. There's often the bonus of that little bit of glaze left in the meat skillet, just enough to moisten and deepen the flavor of the hash you plan to make later in the week. To say nothing of the fact that you can afford to lavish on yourself the occasional rather expensive lobster, or soft-shell crabs, or a rich piece of goose or duck confit (the scraps of which can go into a mini-cassoulet).

Finally, there is something about going home at the end of the day or giving over a quiet Sunday afternoon to cooking—smashing the garlic, chopping an onion, getting all those good cooking smells going, stirring, and tasting mindfully, and then adjusting the seasonings—that makes us feel creative. It is a comforting form of relaxation—something that is needed in our busy lives. I always love the moment of drama, too, when everything comes together and I quickly dish up my handiwork, arranging it pleasingly on a warm plate, and then take it to the table, where I've set a place for one with a cloth napkin in a family napkin ring. I open up the wine and light the candles, turn on some music, and give thanks.

I wouldn't miss this pleasure for anything. And I hope that the strategies and the flexible recipes I offer here will encourage you to join in the fun.

The Pleasures
of Cooking for One

One Cooking Through the Week

Second round: Oxtails with Grits or Polenta

Third round: Penne with a Meaty Sauce

Calf's Liver with Shallot and Wine Pan Sauce

Lemony Scaloppine of Pork

Gratinate of Pork Scaloppine with Eggplant or Zucchini Slices

A Small Roast Pork Tenderloin

Second round: Red Flannel Pork Hash

Pork Stir-Fry with Vegetables

Broiled Lamb Chop with Broiled New Potatoes

Second round: Lamb and Lentils

ABOUT GARLIC

Braised Shoulder Lamb Chops

Moroccan-Style Lamb Shanks with Potatoes and Peas

Second round: Couscous with Lamb, Onions, and Raisins

A Simplified Lamb Curry

Blanquette de Veau with Leeks

Fresh Veal Tongue

A Small Meatloaf with a French Accent

A Slice of Baked Ham

Farm-Raised Snapper with Fennel, Scallions, and Red Pepper

Baked Bass with Fingerlings and Zucchini

Fillet of Fish in Parchment

Fish Cakes

Sautéed Shrimp

Pan-Seared Salmon

Broiled Bluefish or Mackerel over a Bed of Artichoke Hearts and Potatoes

Roasted Branzino (Loup de Mer)

Steamed Mussels

Second round: Chinese Style

Third rounds: On the Half Shell with Dressing

À l'Escargot

The secret of making cooking for one fun and creative is not to think of a meal as self-contained but to understand that home cooking is an ongoing process, one dish leading to another. When I'm doing my major food shopping on the weekend, as most working people do, I visualize the week ahead. What do I have a yen for? How many meals am I going to be eating at home? If I buy this tempting whole tenderloin of pork, I can see using it in at least three different ways: one night, a few slices sautéed in a lemony pan sauce; another, a simple quick roast macerated first in garlic and ginger (any leftovers from that might go into a hash or a rice dish); finally, the thinner end piece cut up for an Asian-type stir-fry with lots of vegetables.

And what about fish? Most cooks feel that it doesn't keep well and has lost its bloom if you try to reincarnate it. But I've found that if I have bought a whole fish or a fillet that's too large for just me, when I use up the leftovers the next day or so in a crispy fish cake, or a fish salad, or combined with other seafood to make a fish soup, a pasta, or a risotto, it comes to life again.

No two of these dishes taste the same, so I never get bored with my leftovers. To me they are like treasures in the fridge that inspire me to do something imaginative as I play with accents from different cuisines. I try, too, to think of a meal in which the vegetables and sometimes the starch are incorporated into the main event. That way it becomes a satisfying meal-in-one-dish to sit down to.

So in this chapter, which I consider the heart of the book, are my main dishes featuring poultry, meats, and fish that have several lives. Nothing is written in stone, however. If you don't happen to have an ingredient that I suggest, try a likely substitute—a shallot for a small onion, some fennel instead of celery, a different root vegetable to replace the ubiquitous carrot, dried mushrooms for fresh. Above all, don't throw away those few tablespoons of cooked spinach, or the three or four extra spears of asparagus you couldn't quite finish, and particularly the little bit of precious juice left in the pan—all these can be used in myriad ways and offer the single home cook some creative challenges.

Essential Equipment When Cooking for One

In making dishes for one, it is crucial to have the right size pans. You can't just reduce a recipe without reducing the dimensions of the utensil in which it is to be cooked. So here are the pans that I call for frequently and which you should have at hand.

A small, heavy pot with cover, 4-cup capacity (I favor Le Creuset), for browning and then braising. This is the pot I use the most.

A large all-purpose 4-quart pan for pasta, stocks, and blanching vegetables

A cast-iron skillet with a bottom diameter of 6 inches, useful for high-heat searing

A larger, nonstick skillet with a bottom diameter of about 8 inches, for larger amounts and stir-fries

A nonstick omelet pan with a bottom diameter of 5½–6½ inches

A small cocotte or other flameproof casserole with lid, 1–1½-cup capacity, that can go on top of the stove and into the oven

A single-portion shallow gratin dish 5 inches in diameter and 1¼ inches deep

A collapsible steamer

A medium-sized strainer

Convenient Extras

A food processor

An immersion blender

A couple of Silpat mats

A small wok with cover

A single-portion tart ring with removable bottom

A single-portion soufflé dish

Poultry shears

A large Chinese mesh spoon, called a "spider," for scooping up pasta or vegetables

A small nutmeg grater

An inexpensive mandoline

A spice grinder

A standing mixer

A small ice cream maker

Some of the cooking pots and pans I use most often, clockwise, starting from above right: a 4-cup Le Creuset pot; a 6-inch cast-iron skillet; inside it, a small ovenproof casserole with lid; a shallow gratin dish; an omelet pan

My favorite knives and a sharpening stone

Indispensable Utensils

A small whisk

A spatula

A pair of tongs

A sturdy wooden spoon or two

A good pepper mill

A box grater

A cheese grater (I much prefer a microplane or a carpenter's rasp)

Excellent knives: minimum of 1 paring knife, 1 chef's knife, and a bread knife

A sharpening stone

Good to Have in the Cupboard

Flours: all-purpose white, whole-wheat, and instant-blending

Baking powder

Baking soda

Cornstarch

Panko (Japanese breadcrumbs)

Sugars: granulated, confectioners', and brown

Salts: table and kosher

Rice: long-grain, short-grain, and wild

Peppercorns

Dried (and canned) beans (see pages 200–204 for suggestions)

Polenta

Pastas of various shapes

Oils: extra-virgin olive oil and light olive or other vegetable oil

Toasted sesame oil

Canned chicken broth

Canned beef broth

Vinegars: red- and white-wine, aged balsamic, and rice

Canned San Marzano tomatoes

Tomato paste (refrigerate after opening)

An assortment of dried herbs and spices (the ones I use most are: bay leaves, curry, *herbes de Provence*, peppercorns, chili pepper flakes, paprika, rosemary, thyme, cinnamon, coriander, cumin, and nutmeg)

Canned tuna fish in olive oil

Canned salmon

Soy sauce

What to Have in the Freezer

Chicken broth or stock
Beef broth or stock
Glace de viande (optional;
   see box, page 83)
Breadcrumbs
Veal, lamb, and duck broth,
   if available
Tomato sauce
Cream sauce
Pesto
Nuts

Sausages
Leftover meat and poultry, raw
   and cooked
Bacon
Surplus fresh vegetables, fruits,
   and berries
Ice cream
Bread dough
Pastry dough
Cookie dough

What to Have in the Refrigerator

Eggs
Butter, preferably unsalted
Heavy cream
Milk
Whole-milk yogurt
Cheese
Dijon mustard
Mayonnaise (Hellmann's Real
   or your own homemade; see
   page 111)
Yeast
In the fruit drawer:
   Oranges, lemons, apples,
     and other seasonal fruits
In the vegetable drawer:
   Scallions, ginger, parsley,
     salad greens (see box,
     page 151)
   Carrots

Red bell pepper
Celery
Mushrooms (best to pack
    them loosely in a large glass
    jar so they can breathe)
Ham and/or prosciutto
Smoked fish
Sausage, dried and fresh
Small jars of your own:
   Pesto (page 158) or green
    sauce (page 159)
   Salad dressing (vinaigrette,
    page 149)
   Meat juice and drippings
Maple syrup, if opened
Jams and/or jellies, if opened
Preserved lemons (see page 241)
Olives
Pickles

Essentials for the Vegetable and Fruit Bins

Onions
Garlic
Unripened fruits
Bananas

Tomatoes
Potatoes, new and
  for baking
Shallots

A Word About Portion Size

I have always found it somewhat presumptuous to prescribe how much anyone should eat at a meal. I feel the yield should be flexible, because it depends so much on the appetite—as well as the age, the sex, the size, and the lifestyle—of those one is feeding. An athletic, young, growing man will happily down three times as much as I can consume, and for him there probably won't be any leftovers to create the second and third rounds I enjoy eating. So, cooking for yourself, you need to treat the recipes I give you in this book only as guidelines and do the arithmetic to suit your needs. My portions reflect what I would serve myself, and they are relatively modest, allowing room for some ripe cheese with a good chunk of bread to be eaten with a salad and/or fruit to round out my dinner.

The Language of Cooking

Cooking is a sensual experience, and you really should allow all your senses full play. Enjoy the feel of ingredients, observe what is happening, taste as you go along, and drink in the heady smells that arouse your anticipation. Then, when you set everything on a plate, even if it's just for you—or especially if it's just for you—make it pleasing to the eye, adding a little color to brighten, if needed.

I feel that the language of recipes should reflect the visceral nature of cooking and invite you to participate more fully, rather than have you slavishly follow a formula. That's why I use expressions like "a pinch of salt," "a splash of wine," "a sprinkling of parsley," "a fat clove of garlic," "a handful of spinach leaves." You don't need to measure that wine precisely. Splash some into the hot pan, let it cook down, if indicated, and then taste. It's a waste of time and too fussy to stuff that bit of chopped parsley into a tablespoon to make sure you have the "right" amount. There are times when exact measures are important, particularly in baking, but even then beware of trying to prepare a bread dough with such rigid precision, because the water content of flour can vary considerably. The only accurate guide is your hands: whether the dough *feels* too sticky or too wet.

I hope that the flexibility I'm encouraging will help you enjoy a more relaxed ease in cooking. Get the feel of a teaspoon of salt by measuring it into your hand before throwing it into the soup pot. Next time, you won't need the teaspoon measure: your hand will tell you the amount. And the more confident you get, the more you will be encouraged to experiment, to try out your own variations of some of these recipes and play with ideas of your own. Cooking for one can be particularly challenging, because often you'll find yourself wanting to reduce recipes for a large number of people to a single portion. So you need to use your wits and your imagination. And if it doesn't work perfectly the first time, try again.

Your hand will tell you.

Broiled Chicken

I use the same technique for broiling a chicken as I do for roasting it whole. I make a tasty mix of shallots, garlic, lemon rind, and herbs moistened with olive oil and rub that under the skin of the chicken at least an hour before cooking. The advantage of broiling is that it's quicker, particularly if you do the preliminary under-the-skin stuffing in the morning. Then, when you get home, you have only to put the accompanying vegetables on a baking tray along with the chicken and you'll have a full dinner ready in 30 minutes with lots of good leftover chicken to play with during the week. You can, of course, just get half a chicken (leg/thigh/breast piece) and have only a little left over, but I find the birds for roasting are apt to be plumper and more flavorful, particularly if you get an organic, decently raised chicken. And I like to have the gizzards, neck, and backbone for stock, and the liver for my own treat (see page 100).

WHAT YOU NEED

1 chicken, about 3 pounds

FOR THE HERBAL UNDERCOATING

1 garlic clove, peeled	A small handful of fresh parsley
Salt	2–3 tablespoons fresh tarragon
1 shallot	leaves, or 1 teaspoon dried
1 scallion	2 tablespoons olive oil
About 2 strips lemon peel	Freshly ground pepper

ACCOMPANYING VEGETABLES

1 carrot	2 or 3 new potatoes
1 parsnip	Olive oil
2 shallots, or 2 thick slices of a small onion, peeled	Salt

Rinse the chicken and pat dry thoroughly with a paper towel. Chop the garlic clove, then sprinkle with ½ teaspoon salt and mash the two together with the flat side of your large knife until you have a paste. Chop the shallot, scallion, lemon peel, parsley, and tarragon, and mix in with the garlic; then mince all together with the olive oil. Add pepper generously.

At least 1 hour before cooking, or the morning of the evening you plan to cook, prepare the chicken. I like to cut out the backbone and save it for stock, as well as trim the wing tips. But instead, you can simply cut the chicken in half, slicing down firmly along the center of the breastbone, using poultry shears (if you have them) to cut through the bone. Or buy the chicken already cut in two pieces. Loosen the skin from the breast and thighs and legs of the chicken, and spread equal amounts of undercoating under the skin on both halves of the chicken, using your fingers to push it down onto the legs and thighs. Rub a little oil onto the nonskin side, and season all over with salt and pepper. Refrigerate until ready to cook.

Preheat the broiler.

Peel the carrot and parsnip, and cut in half lengthwise; cut the shallots in half, and the potatoes in thirds. Spread the pieces on a roasting pan; or simply line a pan sheet with Silpat, rub a little olive oil on, and roll the vegetables in that. Salt lightly. Place the chicken halves, skin side down, in the center, with the vegetables around, and set on a rack about 6 inches under the broiler. Watch the vegetables and turn them now and then, tucking under the chicken any pieces that start to char. Baste after 5 minutes with a little olive oil. After 20 minutes, turn the chicken and broil the other side, basting this time with the pan juices. It will need another 15 minutes on this side. Remove some of the vegetables if they are cooking too much, and keep warm. The chicken should be done in 35 minutes, but you should check by pricking deeply into where the thigh attaches to the breast to make sure the juices run clear. If you have an instant-read thermometer, plunge it into that area; the temperature should be about 165°. Let rest for 5 minutes before giving yourself a handsome serving of either leg-thigh or breast, along with any pan juice and the roasted vegetables.

Variations

ROAST ROCK CORNISH HEN

You can broil or roast a hen in the same way, first rubbing the undercoating under the skin. A 2-pounder, which is what you usually find in the supermarket today, will take about 30 minutes to cook. Recently I discovered that Bell & Evans was offering a small 1-pounder—the way Cornish hens used to be. It took less than 25 minutes to cook and was delicious. Use proportionately less herbal undercoating for the smaller birds.

WHOLE ROAST CHICKEN

Stuff it under the skin the same way as described for the Broiled Chicken, and rub a little salt and olive oil over it. There's no need to truss the bird. Put it in a roasting pan, breast side down, and roast in a preheated 375° oven for 45 minutes, basting once or twice, then turn the bird so it is breast side up, and roast another 30 minutes, basting a few times. Check for doneness as described on page 15. Let rest for 5 minutes before carving.

Second and Third Rounds—and More

Cold chicken is always good to have around for sandwiches and salads. But here are two of my favorite old-fashioned recipes that make use of leftover chicken in particularly pleasing ways. If you're looking for more ideas, see "The Nine Lives of a Turkey" (box, pages 22–23). What you can do with turkey almost always applies to chicken, too.

Chicken Divan

⅔ cup Cream Sauce (page 164), defrosted if frozen

1 tablespoon or more chicken broth

1 tablespoon dry sherry

½ bunch broccolini

Salt and freshly ground pepper

3 tablespoons freshly grated Parmesan cheese

3 slices cooked chicken breast, plus several scraps

Preheat the oven to 375°.

Warm the cream sauce slowly, beat it thoroughly, and thin it with the broth and sherry until it is the consistency of a medium-thick soup.

Using a vegetable peeler, shave off the outer skin from the broccolini stems. Cut each whole branch in thirds. Put the stem pieces in a steamer basket set over boiling water, and steam for 2 minutes; then add the florets, and steam another 2 minutes.

Spread the broccolini on the bottom of a single-serving shallow gratin dish about 6 inches in diameter. Salt and pepper lightly, drizzle about 2 tablespoons of the cream sauce over it, and sprinkle on 1 tablespoon of the Parmesan. Lay the chicken pieces on top, and tuck in a few extra scraps around the edge. Salt and pepper lightly again, and spread the remaining sauce over the top. Sprinkle on the rest of the cheese, bake for 25 minutes, then run under the broiler just long enough to brown the top.

Second Round

Minced Chicken on Toast

Minces were quite popular in nineteenth-century American cooking. I often had minced chicken and turkey and sometimes lamb on toast as a child, and I always loved the simple, soothing flavor of those dishes. If you haven't got cream sauce on hand, just use cream and let it cook down a little.

2 teaspoons butter

2 or 3 button mushrooms or
   cremini, finely chopped

1 scallion, finely chopped

1 tablespoon Madeira

¾–1 cup cooked chicken, cut into
   very small pieces—i.e., minced

Salt and freshly ground pepper

¼ cup Cream Sauce (page 164),
   or 2 tablespoons heavy cream

1 slice good white bread or
   English muffin, toasted

A sprinkling of tarragon, fresh or
   dried

Melt the butter in a small pan, and add the mushrooms and scallion. Cook gently for about 5 minutes, to soften. Splash in the Madeira, and cook down until syrupy.

Add the chicken, season with salt and pepper, and heat through, stirring in enough of the cream sauce to bind the chicken or use heavy cream. Spoon everything over toast, and sprinkle a little tarragon on top.

I like to surround my mince with a green vegetable, such as asparagus or peas when in season.

Variations

This mince is good made with the remains of a holiday turkey, and if you have some chestnuts left over, by all means use a couple of them, roughly chopped, in place of the mushrooms.

Another accompaniment I tried recently was some young milkweed pods, their tender leaves and buds still closed. I steamed them for about 8 minutes, then bathed them in sweet butter and a few drops of lemon. It made for an early-summer treat, just right with an old-fashioned New England mince.

Chicken Breast (or Leg-Thigh Pieces) Sautéed

People often asked me, as I was writing this book, What should I do with chicken breasts? I think they want to cook chicken breasts because they are lean (therefore supposedly good for you) and quick to prepare, but there's that persistent problem that there are inevitably two to a package, too much for a single meal. Frankly, I see that not as a problem but as an asset, because, again, you have something to play with for a second round. Here is a basic recipe for cooking the chicken so that it is flavorful and not dried out; it can be varied in as many ways as there are vegetables in season. I confess that I prefer dark chicken meat over light; if you feel the same way, just substitute two leg-thigh pieces for the breast meat, and cook about 5 minutes longer.

WHAT YOU NEED

1 whole chicken breast, split and boned, preferably with skin left on

Salt and freshly ground pepper

1 tablespoon butter

¼ bell pepper, red, orange, or purple, cut into matchsticks

1 small zucchini, cut into matchsticks

4 scallions (or more if very thin), cut into matchsticks

A splash of white wine

A sprinkling of parsley or other fresh seasonal herbs

If the packaged breast meat you buy has not been boned, it is very easy to do yourself. Simply use a sharp knife to scrape the breast meat off the rib cage and free the wishbone, if it's still there. Save the bones for soup.

Rinse the chicken, and pat dry thoroughly with paper towels. Rub salt and pepper over both sides. Heat the butter in an 8- or 9-inch heavy skillet, and lay in the chicken. Let brown over medium heat for about 3 minutes, then turn and brown the other side. Continue to sauté for

15 minutes, turning several times, then push the chicken to the edge of the pan. Remove all but 2 teaspoons of the fat, toss the bell pepper into the bare part of the pan, and stir-fry for 2 minutes. Add the zucchini and scallions and continue to cook, tossing and stirring, until they are just tender—about 3 minutes more. Sprinkle on more salt to taste and a few grindings of pepper. Remove one of the chicken pieces to a warm plate and surround it with the vegetables (setting the other piece of chicken aside for a second round). Turn the heat up a little, and splash some wine into the pan. When it has reduced and thickened slightly, spoon out the pan juice, scraping up any brown bits, and pour it over the chicken you are about to eat. Sprinkle some parsley or other herbs on top.

Variations

Try other vegetable combinations: artichoke hearts with slices of onion and new potatoes; root vegetables such as parsnips, celery root, and young turnips are all good with strips of peppers; play with mushrooms, shallots, and fennel, as well as broccoli florets or broccolini. Longer-cooking vegetables are better blanched first for several minutes.

Second Rounds

Cold chicken always lends itself to a good chicken sandwich or salad (see suggestions, pages 146 and 147). Leftover breast meat is nice in a Greek soup (see page 89).

The Nine Lives of a Turkey

I often think of the remark made by Edna Lewis, the author of the incomparable *The Taste of Country Cooking,* about her Virginia childhood: that having a country ham in the refrigerator is like owning a good black dress—you are ready for anything. I feel that way when the holiday dinner is over and the remains of a fat turkey are occupying a good deal of space in my fridge. To me it's like a secret treasure I can draw on in the days to come, to improvise a meal for myself or anyone who may turn up hungry. But there's also a challenge to it: I don't want to get tired of the taste of turkey. So I'm determined to give that bird nine very different lives.

As I imagine its possible reincarnations, I am drawn back to the past, to the kind of dishes that were part of every family's repertoire when I was growing up, and my mouth begins to water as I think of recovering some of those taste memories.

First, I scrape the remaining meat from the carcass, bagging separately the dark and white slices and miscellaneous chunks. All the bones with some small nuggets of meat still clinging to them go into a large pot with an onion or two, a couple of celery ribs, a carrot, some leek leaves, if I have them, and some parsley stems, which I always have around. I pour cold water over it all, to cover by at least an inch, salt lightly, and let the brew cook slowly for about 4 hours. That will give me not only a couple of quarts of turkey stock to freeze, but also the makings of my first meal.

RICH TURKEY SOUP   I heat up a few ladles of the broth and stir in some leftover stuffing (there's always some clinging to the cavity, and you need only enough to thicken and flavor the broth). Then I toss in some ribbons of salad greens (trimmed from escarole, romaine, or whatever else I have), and maybe a chunk of toasted bread, and sprinkle a generous grating of Parmesan on top.

TURKEY TETTRAZINI   An old family favorite, much like Chicken Divan (page 17). You can follow that recipe, but substitute three or four sautéed sliced mushrooms for the broccolini.

WILD RICE PILAF WITH TURKEY   I served wild rice with my holiday turkey, but you can use any cooked rice to put together this meal-in-one dish (see page 178).

TURKEY, VEGETABLE, AND CHEESE STRATA OR SAVORY CUSTARD Use a couple of slices of turkey to make a creamy baked strata for one (see page 113).

WALDORF SALAD   Remember that one? It's made of apple, celery, walnuts, and chicken. I like to vary it with slices of fennel and, of course, turkey. There are other ideas for salads in which you can replace chicken with turkey (see pages 146 and 147).

TURKEY CROQUETTES   Mix ¼ cup cream sauce with ½ cup minced turkey and a chopped scallion. Season well and form into a patty. Dredge in flour, then beaten egg, then breadcrumbs, and fry. For more detail, see my recipe for croquettes in *The Tenth Muse*.

A TURKEY SANDWICH   It's hard to beat slices of turkey breast with lettuce and lots of mayonnaise spread right to the edges of some good white bread. But sometimes I'll vary it with grilled red pepper on top, or a thin slice of broiled eggplant. And you can use different kinds of grilled vegetables.

TURKEY CRÊPES   If I have some crêpe batter (see page 230) on hand, and a few dollops of cream sauce in the freezer, it is simple to make a couple of thin crêpes and stuff them with some finely chopped turkey meat bound together by the cream sauce and seasoned with some scallions and maybe a bit of mushroom duxelles (page 138).

TURKEY CHESTNUT HASH   I am coming to the end of my turkey and thinking hash, or a mince, as this kind of dish was often called in the past. I have only dark meat left, and that is really best for hash. If you've used chestnuts for stuffing your bird and have a few left, you can make a particularly delicious mince of turkey and chestnuts. Follow the recipe for Minced Chicken on Toast (page 18).

Skirt Steak

This is my favorite steak. I like the chewiness of the cut and the faint marbling of fat, just enough to keep it well lubricated. And I find it a good size for the single cook. A skirt steak of approximately 14 ounces gives me three fine meals. First I have a piece of rare steak quickly sautéed and garnished with a little pan sauce of wine and shallots; then I have a few slices of it cold for lunch with a piquant sauce; and finally, later in the week, I'll use what remains in a delicious baked dish with mushrooms and breadcrumbs, an inspiration of the late Mireille Johnston, whose books taught us so much of what regional French home cooking is all about—thriftiness, inventiveness, and good taste.

WHAT YOU NEED

1 or 2 garlic cloves, smashed and peeled

Salt

About ½ teaspoon fresh ginger, peeled and grated (optional)

Freshly ground pepper

A skirt steak of about 14 ounces, preferably grass-fed

Light olive oil

1 tablespoon butter

1 fat shallot, finely chopped

¼ cup red wine

A sprinkling of chopped fresh parsley

Chop the garlic fine, then sprinkle on about ¼ teaspoon of salt, and with the flat of your knife, mash the two together until you have a paste. Mix the ginger into the paste, if you're using it—it isn't French, but it adds a *je ne sais quoi* that's delicious. Sprinkle on several generous grindings of pepper, rub this paste onto both sides of the steak, and cut it in thirds or in half, so that it will fit into your skillet. Smear just a little oil on the bottom of a heavy 8-inch skillet, and heat until almost smoking, then lay in the steak and sear over high heat for 1 minute on each side. Now put the pan in a preheated 350° oven for about 4 minutes (or more if you don't want it rare). Remove the steak to a warm plate while you quickly make the sauce. Swirl the butter in the hot skillet, and sauté the shallot for a minute. Splash in the wine, and reduce by half. Pour the sauce over the portion of the steak you are going to eat immediately. Top with some chopped parsley.

Second Round

BEEF WITH SAUCE GRIBICHE

Even better than a steak sandwich is a plate of thinly sliced rare beef with Sauce Gribiche spooned over and a garnish of cucumbers and small tomatoes. I first experienced this sauce at a little brasserie on the rue de Seine in Paris and immediately went home to work out the ingredients and create my own version. There are many variations (mine is on page 160), and it's a sauce to treasure, because it enhances so many cold meats, especially the organ meats I relish, as well as fish.

Herbs and Spices

Herbs can be a problem for the cook living alone—or, for that matter, for any cook today. So many recipes, particularly from chefs, call for two or three different fresh herbs—a sprig of fresh thyme, two fresh bay leaves or sage leaves, several tablespoons of chopped chives, for example—and by the time you've invested in three packets of herbs, you've spent as much on seasoning your meat as you did for the meat. Moreover, the herbs that you buy aren't particularly fresh, smothered as they are in envelopes of plastic, so you're apt to throw out the limp remains.

One solution is to substitute dried herbs, which good cooks have been doing for ages. There's no hard and fast formula for dried versus fresh, but in general start with about four times the amount of fresh herbs as you would dried, and taste—you can always add more.

Make sure that your dried herbs aren't stale. Buy them in small quantities, date them, and replace them at least once a year. It's helpful to have a spice grinder, too, so that you can buy the whole seeds of spices like coriander, cardamom, and cumin (which you probably won't use that often) and grind them to order.

Always buy a whole dried nutmeg and grate it on a little grater made for that purpose. You can also use the fine holes of a box grater.

It goes without saying that you need a good pepper mill to grind pepper fresh to order. And a useful piece of advice I learned from chef Scott Peacock: never keep your pepper grinder on the shelf above your stove; the peppercorns will dry out with the heat and taste stale.

Another strategy is to grow a few fresh herbs in pots on a sunny windowsill, if you have one. I like to keep pots of parsley, small-leaved basil, tarragon, and rosemary going as long as I can. And I'm lucky in summer because I do have a garden in northern Vermont. Even then, in that cool climate, I often have to bring my basil plants in at night.

Third Round

Gratin of Beef, Mushrooms, and Breadcrumbs

WHAT YOU NEED

A half-dozen medium
  mushrooms
1 garlic clove, peeled
1 shallot
2 tablespoons fresh
  breadcrumbs, plus more for
  topping

2 tablespoons chopped fresh
  parsley
Salt and freshly ground pepper
Light olive oil
3 or 4 fairly thin slices leftover
  steak
A splash of red wine

Chop the mushrooms, garlic, and shallot into small dice, and mix with the breadcrumbs and parsley. Salt and pepper generously. Smear a little oil on the bottom of a shallow one-serving gratin dish, and spread half of the mushroom mixture on the bottom. Cover that with three or four slices of the remaining skirt steak, and sprinkle a little red wine over it all; salt again lightly. Finish with a layer of the remaining mushroom mixture. For the topping, sprinkle a scant tablespoon of breadcrumbs over it all, and drizzle on a bit of olive oil. Bake at 375° for 25 minutes.

Good Beef Raised Close to Home

In my memoir about my life in food, *The Tenth Muse,* I wrote about the venture that my stepdaughter, Bronwyn, and I had recently embarked on: raising grass-fed beef with my cousin John Reynolds, who farms in northern Vermont. The idea was to have a very small herd eating off our lands, supplemented by large amounts of hay that John harvested during the summer. When we invested in our first six Angus cows I hadn't fully realized what a pleasure it would be to see our fields returning to good pasturelands and to look out at our well-nurtured cattle grazing contentedly and nursing their young.

Recently I tasted the meat of the first round that had gone to market, and as I bit into the loin we had roasted, it was so good I found myself near tears. I hadn't enjoyed meat like this since I first went to Paris in my twenties, and at a little inexpensive bistro ate an entrecôte from farm-raised local cattle—slightly chewy but intensely beefy tasting. It made me realize what I'd been missing at home in America; the flavor had gone out of our beef. As I took a second bite of our loin roast, I felt overwhelmed with gratitude to John and his family for the loving care they had given our small herd and for the cows themselves, whose meat was a testament to the good life they had led. I was more than ever convinced that the way in which animals are raised, the natural food they consume, and even the way they are slaughtered accounts for the goodness of their meat.

So I urge those of you cooking just for yourself to seek out reliable sources of food, particularly meat and poultry. Granted, it costs a little more, but then you can compensate by eating less the first time around and stretching what's left by marrying it with aromatic vegetables and earthy accompaniments as good cooks the world over have done for centuries.

Boeuf Bourguignon

Make this rich stew on a leisurely weekend. You'll probably get a good three meals out of it, if you follow some of the suggestions below. When buying stew meat at a supermarket, you don't always know what you are getting, so ask the butcher. If it's a lean meat, it will need less time cooking (in fact, it will be ruined if you cook it too long), but the fattier cuts can benefit from at least another half hour.

WHAT YOU NEED

2 ounces bacon, cut into small pieces, preferably a chunk cut into little dice

About 1¼ pounds beef stew meat, cut into 1- to 1½-inch pieces

1 tablespoon light olive oil

1 medium onion, diced

⅓ carrot, thick end, peeled and diced

2 teaspoons all-purpose flour

Salt

1 cup red wine

1 cup beef broth

Herb packet of ½ bay leaf; a fat garlic clove, smashed; a small handful of parsley stems; ¼ teaspoon dried thyme; 4 or 5 peppercorns

VEGETABLE GARNISH

3 or 4 baby onions, or four 1-inch pieces of leek

3 or 4 baby carrots, or the thin ends of larger ones, peeled

2 or 3 small new potatoes

Brown the bacon in a heavy pot, fairly deep but not too large. When it has released its fat and is lightly browned, remove it to a dish, leaving the fat in the pan. Pat the pieces of beef dry with a paper towel. Pour the oil into the pot, and when it is hot, brown half the pieces of beef on all sides. Remove to the plate with the bacon, and brown the remaining pieces. Now sauté the onion and the carrot until they are lightly browned. Return the meats to the pot, sprinkle on the flour and some salt, and pour the wine and beef stock in. Tuck the herb packet into the pot, and bring to a boil; then reduce the heat, cover, and cook at a lively simmer for about 1 hour or more, depending on the cut of the meat. Bite into a piece to determine if it is almost done (it will get another 20 minutes or so of cooking with the vegetables).

When the time is right, add all the vegetables, cover, and cook at a lively simmer again for 20–25 minutes—pierce the veggies to see if they are tender. Serve yourself four or five chunks of meat, with all the vegetables, and a good French bread to mop up the sauce.

Second Round

Use three or four pieces and some of the remaining sauce to make a quick Beef and Kidney Pie (page 34) later in the week. The recipe follows Veal Kidneys in Mustard Sauce because you want to use the leftover kidneys to put this dish together.

Third Round

Use what remains to make a meaty pasta sauce for one, breaking up the meat and adding three or four squeezed San Marzano plum tomatoes. Simmer the sauce as the pasta cooks.

Veal Kidneys in Mustard Sauce

Every now and then I get a yearning for this dish, which you'll readily find in almost any little bistro in Paris. The Dijon mustard is the perfect complement to the earthiness of the kidneys, and it is a particularly comforting dish to savor on a raw winter day. Kidneys seem to be increasingly hard to come by in our markets today, so when you see them, bring them home. Even if you think you don't like rognons de veau, *I beg you to try cooking them this way. I think you'll be converted.*

Recently I asked the butcher at Citarella, a first-rate purveyor in New York City, if he had veal kidneys. Sure enough, he found some in the chiller below. But the one he brought up and proudly showed me turned out to weigh just over a pound (most veal kidneys are 7–9 ounces untrimmed). Still, I couldn't resist, and as I thought of how I might use up what remained, a vision of a little beef and kidney pie, which my mother used to serve occasionally, popped into my mind (recipe follows). I'd quickly decided to make it with some good leftover Boeuf Bourguignon (preceding recipe), so I also purchased a pound of stewing meat and went home planning my dinners for the week ahead.

WHAT YOU NEED

1 veal kidney, about 1 pound
   or less

2 teaspoons butter

1 teaspoon light olive oil

1 shallot, chopped fine

¼ cup white wine or vermouth

2 teaspoons fresh lemon juice

1 heaping tablespoon Dijon
   mustard mashed into
   1 tablespoon soft butter

Salt and freshly ground pepper

A scattering of chopped fresh
   parsley

Rinse the kidney and dry it. Cut out all the fat from the underside, remove any heavy membrane that's been left on, then flatten out the kidney. Heat the butter and oil in a heavy sauté pan about the size of the kidney, and when the fat is sizzling, with the large bubbles beginning to break up, lay in the kidney, and cook over moderate to high heat for 12 minutes, turning it over once, watching the heat carefully so that it remains hot but does not burn. Remove the kidney to a warm plate, and cover to keep warm.

Sauté the shallot in the pan fat for about a minute, then add the wine and lemon juice, and reduce, scraping up the browned bits, until the pan juices are syrupy. Turn off the heat, and whisk in the mustard-butter about ½ teaspoon at a time. Now you can either slice the kidney in fairly thick slices or break it up in lobes, and return the pieces to the pan with any accumulated juice, leaving them there just long enough to heat up. Salt and pepper to taste, turning the kidneys in the sauce to season evenly. Set aside the portion you want to save for your Beef and Kidney Pie (recipe follows), and sprinkle a little parsley on your immediate serving. Enjoy it with some rice or polenta.

Second Round

Beef and Kidney Pie

WHAT YOU NEED

Leftover veal kidneys, 3 or
    4 lobes
Leftover Boeuf Bourguignon
    (page 31), 3 or 4 pieces
Leftover sauce from both

Thickener, either instant flour or
    beurre manié (see procedure),
    as needed
Salt and freshly ground pepper
3 ounces Pastry Dough (page 226)

Preheat the oven to 425°.

Put the sauce from the kidneys and from the beef into a small saucepan and heat. If it seems too thin, thicken it with a small amount of instant flour (about ½ teaspoon in a ½ cup of liquid), or, better still, massage about ½ teaspoon of flour into a teaspoon of butter, and drop a little bit at a time into the sauce, whisking, until it is lightly thickened. This may not be necessary if your cooking liquid is thick enough—about the consistency of a good gravy.

Arrange the meats in a small casserole or baking dish, 2 inches deep and 5 inches in diameter. Pour the sauce over, taste, and add salt and pepper if necessary. Roll out the dough to a circle 6 inches in diameter or a little more, then roll it up on the rolling pin and drape it over the baking dish. Curl the dough that hangs over, and pinch it firmly all around the edge. Make two or three slashes on top, and bake in the preheated oven for 10 minutes, then turn down the heat to 375° and cook 10–15 minutes more, until lightly golden on top, with the juices bubbling through the slashes.

Beef Shank and Oxtail Ragù

This is something I'm tempted to make when my supply of rich beef broth is low. But maybe that's an excuse. The truth is, I love eating these cuts, spooning out the marrow from the shank, and, in the second dish, sucking off meat from the little tail bones. It's nice, messy eating, perhaps best enjoyed alone with a kitchen towel around one's neck. I usually still have some meat left after lapping up these two dishes—just enough to make myself a pasta on a night when I want a quick supper. Then there's the treasure of the rich beef broth to put away.

WHAT YOU NEED

1 tablespoon light olive oil or
    duck or goose fat
Salt
About 1½ pounds oxtails
A large beef shank, about
    1¼ pounds
1 large onion, chopped

1 large carrot, peeled and chopped
½ cup red wine
Herb packet of a dozen or so
    parsley stems, 1 garlic clove,
    1 bay leaf, ½ teaspoon dried
    thyme, 8 peppercorns
7–8 cups water

VEGETABLES FOR THE FIRST TIME AROUND

4 small white onions, peeled

3 or 4 young carrots, peeled and
    cut into ½-inch pieces

½ medium white turnip, or
    ¼ fairly large celery root,

peeled and cut into chunks
    (optional)

2 or 3 smallish new potatoes,
    cut in half

Heat the oil or fat in a heavy pot. Salt the meats lightly, and brown on all sides. Remove the meat (or push it aside if your pot is big enough), and sauté the onion and carrot for a few minutes. Splash in the red wine and reduce for a minute, then tuck the meat back in among the vegetables, nestling in the herb packet as well. Pour on enough water to cover the meats by 2 inches, and simmer, covered, for 2½ hours. Add the additional vegetables, and a little more water if they are not well covered, and simmer until tender—about 20 minutes.

For my first meal, I have the shank surrounded by the vegetables with a little of the cooking liquid on top. If I have some on hand, a Winter Green Sauce (page 159) is particularly good with this. I reserve for later any meat I can't finish.

Second Round

OXTAILS WITH GRITS OR POLENTA

Spoon most of the oxtails into a warm wide, shallow bowl into which you've dished up a generous serving of grits or polenta (see pages 196 and 193). Pour a small ladleful of the flavorful beef broth over, thickened, if you like, with a little cornstarch or instant flour. If you want to jazz up the dish, make a small amount of the gremolata (see page 249) that is used for veal shanks—just a teaspoon sprinkled on top is enough.

PENNE WITH A MEATY SAUCE

Bring a large pot of salted water to a boil, and start cooking 2–3 ounces of penne or ziti. Meanwhile, scrape off from the bones whatever meat remains, and chop it up. Strain the rich cooking broth into containers for freezing, reserving the vegetables. Heat a little olive oil in a medium skillet, and lightly sauté a thin-sliced garlic clove for a minute. Add the strained veggies, the chopped-up meat, and about ¼ cup tomato sauce (or, if you don't have any, use a tablespoon tomato paste and some of the pasta water). Scoop up the pasta when done, and mix it with the sauce in the skillet, adding more pasta water if needed. Turn off the heat, and fold in a small handful of grated Parmesan.

Calf's Liver with Shallot and Wine Pan Sauce

I can't resist a piece of calf's liver when I see it—all too infrequently—in the meat counter. It's even better if you get it from a considerate butcher who will cut an even-sized ¼-inch slice and spare you the finicky job of removing the outside membrane.

Liver in a winey sauce is particularly good on a cold winter night; somehow I always feel my red corpuscles are strengthened by its rich meatiness. I like it with some potatoes alongside. If you have a couple of cooked potatoes, you can brown them in a little butter while the liver cooks, or if you don't have them on hand, try grating a medium raw potato through the coarse holes of a grinder and make a quick potato pancake.

WHAT YOU NEED

A generous sprinkling of all-purpose flour

Salt

1 tablespoon butter

A slice of liver, ¼-inch thick

1 fat shallot, finely chopped

2 good splashes of red wine

Freshly ground pepper

A scattering of chopped parsley leaves

Sprinkle the flour and a pinch of salt on a piece of wax paper. Dredge the liver, cut into two pieces if it is large, in the flour. Heat 1 teaspoon of the butter in a small heavy skillet over moderately high heat. When it starts to sizzle, drop the liver into the pan. Sauté quickly, still over quite high heat, for about 1 minute on each side, then remove to a plate. Clean out the burned butter left in the pan, let the pan cool a little, and melt the remaining butter over moderate heat. Toss in the shallot. Cook, stirring, until it softens, and splash a little wine into the pan. Let it reduce quickly and then add another splash and return the liver to the pan. Cook to warm through. Check to see if the liver is done to your liking by cutting into a piece; I like it still rosy. Salt and pepper the liver lightly, remove to a warm plate, spooning the shallot and pan sauce over it, and sprinkle parsley on top.

Second Round

I find the usual supermarket-packaged piece of liver too big for me so I set aside a piece, about 2 ounces, to make an unusual and delicious pasta (see page 182).

I like to buy a whole pork tenderloin, weighing about 1¼ pounds, and use it in three or four different ways during the week. Don't be fooled by how they are shrink-wrapped in the supermarket; there are usually two tenderloins nestled together in one package, and all you want is one for yourself. So take it to the butcher and ask him to open it up and sell you just the one. It pays to be persistent. First, I'll make myself some quick scaloppine (I offer two treatments below, so that you can have some variety), then I'll cut off the thin end and set aside about 2 ounces to go into a stir-fry. The bulk of the pork I roast, and if there's some left over from that, it goes into a hash. Here are the guidelines.

Lemony Scaloppine of Pork

I like this in winter with rice, or with mashed potatoes mixed, maybe, with mashed parsnip or another root vegetable. In summer, it's good with almost anything from the garden.

WHAT YOU NEED

3 thin slices pork tenderloin
Salt and freshly ground pepper
All-purpose flour for dredging
1 teaspoon light olive oil
2 teaspoons butter
4 very thin slices lemon, plus
  ½ lemon for squeezing

1 fat shallot, sliced paper-thin
2–3 tablespoons chicken broth
  or water
1½ teaspoons capers, rinsed
A scattering of chopped fresh
  parsley

Place your very sharp chef's knife flat on top of the pork tenderloin about 2½ inches from the thicker end. Tilting the knife slightly on the diagonal,

Lemony Scaloppine of Pork continued

slice off one quite thin scallop, moving from where you inserted the knife toward and off the end. Repeat two more times to make three slices. Pound the scallops gently to an even thickness, salt and pepper them lightly, and dredge them in flour. Heat the oil in a skillet just large enough for the three scaloppine, then add the butter, and when it is sizzling, lay in the meat along with the slices of lemon and shallot. Cook the scallops over medium-high heat for less than a minute on each side, then remove to a warm plate. Squeeze most of the half-lemon into the pan, add the chicken broth (or water), and boil down until lightly thickened. Toss in the capers, and return the meat to the pan just to heat through. Taste to see if it needs a little more lemon and/or salt. Spoon everything onto your warm plate, and scatter a little parsley on top.

Gratinate of Pork Scaloppine with Eggplant or Zucchini Slices

Instead of making the lemon scaloppine, try this delightful dish from Lidia Bastianich, in which the vegetables almost take center stage and the meat is an accent. It is important in reducing this recipe to one serving to use a small pan so that the sauce does not evaporate.

1 small eggplant, about 6 inches
long, or a small zucchini
Salt and freshly ground pepper
All-purpose flour for dredging
1–2 tablespoons light olive oil
3 ounces pork tenderloin
1 tablespoon butter
1 shallot, minced
A splash of white wine

About 6 fresh basil leaves
3–4 tablespoons tomato sauce or
2 teaspoons tomato paste
diluted with ¼ cup water
3 tablespoons freshly grated
Parmesan
½ cup veal, beef, or chicken
stock, homemade or a
substitute (see page 83)

Trim the stem off the eggplant. Slice a wide strip of skin off lengthwise on either side and discard, then slice the eggplant lengthwise into ¼-inch slices. Salt and pepper them, and dredge lightly in flour. (If you are using zucchini, cut it into diagonal ¼-inch slices and dredge them.) Heat 1 tablespoon of the olive oil in a 6-inch frying pan, and lightly brown the eggplant slices on both sides, adding a little more oil if necessary. Remove to paper towels. Cut scallop-sized pieces of pork (see procedure in preceding recipe), and flatten them between sheets of wax paper, then salt and pepper lightly and dredge in flour. Add the butter to the pan, and sauté the pork for a minute or two on each side. Remove from the pan, and set aside with the eggplant. Toss in the shallot, sauté briefly, then splash in the wine and let it almost boil away. Put the pieces of meat back in the skillet in one layer, with leaves of basil laid over them, then arrange the slices of eggplant on top, and spoon about 1 tablespoon of the tomato sauce over each piece. Sprinkle the cheese over it, and drizzle just a little tomato sauce in the bottom of the pan, along with the stock. Bake in a preheated 400° oven for 8–10 minutes, or until the meat is tender when poked and there is still a little sauce left in the pan.

A Small Roast Pork Tenderloin

I give a garlic-ginger coating to the portion of the pork I'm going to roast. It should be applied at least an hour before roasting, but I usually do it in the morning of the day I'm going to roast the tenderloin. This is particularly good with some roasted vegetables surrounding the pork—halved small new potatoes, a root vegetable such as a white turnip cut in half, a few slices of celery root, a split parsnip, or some chunks of winter squash. Rub them in light olive oil first, salt lightly, then scatter in a small roasting pan around the pork. If they aren't quite done when the pork is, turn up the heat and give them another 5 minutes or so while the meat is resting.

WHAT YOU NEED

1 fat garlic clove, peeled

1 teaspoon kosher salt

1 teaspoon Dijon mustard

1 teaspoon grated fresh ginger

1 pork tenderloin, trimmed as
   described on page 39

Freshly ground pepper

A handful of the vegetables
   suggested above

Chop the garlic clove fine, then sprinkle on the salt and mash with the flat of your big knife. Smear the mustard, the mashed garlic, and the ginger over both sides of the pork, and pepper generously. Refrigerate until you are ready to roast.

Preheat the oven to 375° and place the little tenderloin in the middle of a roasting pan, with whatever vegetables you are roasting scattered around it. Roast for 30 minutes, then remove the meat and let rest for 5 or 10 minutes, while you finish the vegetables. Make a handsome plate of slices of pork with the veggies all around.

Second Round

Red Flannel Pork Hash

From cooking a corned beef hash lunch with Julia Child, I learned a few tips about what makes a really delicious hash, whether it be made with cooked lamb, beef, poultry, or, in this case, pork. I discovered the importance of adding some stock and cooking the hash slowly at first, to form a glaze, and of always cutting the meat in small pieces, never grinding. You use approximately the same amount of meat as potatoes, and it's essential to include some aromatic vegetables to give off their sweetness and help form the glaze that makes the crust. I am using a cooked beet here, because New Englanders always include it with pork—hence the name "red flannel"—but use other handy vegetables, such as mushrooms, red peppers, carrot, or fennel, that are good foils for whatever meat you have left over. I cook it all in my sturdy 8-inch cast-iron pan, which I think is better than nonstick for a hash.

WHAT YOU NEED

1 tablespoon butter or duck or goose fat

½ medium onion, chopped

1 small rib celery, chopped

2 medium-small new potatoes, cooked, peeled and diced

1 small beet, roasted or boiled, peeled and diced

3 ounces cooked pork, chopped

¼ cup stock (beef, veal, goose— whatever's on hand)

Salt and freshly ground pepper

Chopped fresh parsley

Melt the butter in a small heavy pan. Stir in the onion and celery, and cook gently until slightly softened, about 5 minutes. Add the potatoes, beet, pork, and stock. Salt and pepper lightly, and cook slowly, covered, over low heat. Remove the cover, and let the bottom brown. Watch carefully, because it can easily blacken. When it is browned, press down firmly with an ample spatula, turn the whole hash over (probably in two or three pieces), and brown the other side. Transfer to a warm plate, and sprinkle a little parsley on top—and enjoy a lovely, nostalgic-tasting supper.

Other aromatic vegetables you might use: carrots or other root vegetables, cut in very fine dice; a couple of button mushrooms, chopped; an equal amount of fennel in place of the celery rib.

Pork Stir-Fry with Vegetables

This is a very flexible stir-fry, so have fun with what you want to mix and match. The important thing is to get everything prepped ahead of time and lined up on a tray near the stove. Have your sauce ingredients mixed in a little bowl, and be sure to have your cooked rice ready.

WHAT YOU NEED

- 1½ tablespoons vegetable oil
- 1 garlic clove, smashed and peeled
- 1 slice ginger about the size of a quarter, peeled
- 2½–3 ounces pork tenderloin, cut into ¼-inch pieces or small strips
- 3 or 4 mushrooms, thick-sliced

- 1 small rib celery, cut into ¼-inch pieces
- About six ¼-inch strips red bell pepper
- 1 tablespoon dry sherry
- ¼ cup chicken broth or water
- 1 small handful of snow peas, strings removed, cut in half on the diagonal

SAUCE

- 2 teaspoons soy sauce
- Pinch of salt
- Pinch of sugar

- 1 teaspoon cornstarch
- 1 tablespoon water

½ teaspoon toasted sesame oil
A scattering of cashews or
    macadamia nuts (optional)

Heat a wok, if you have one; otherwise, use a fairly large skillet. Pour in half the oil, and when it's hot, scatter in the garlic and ginger. Swirl for half a minute, then toss in the pork, and stir-fry over high heat for less than a minute. Remove the meat to a bowl, and pour the remaining oil into the wok. Toss in the mushrooms, celery, and bell pepper, and stir-fry another minute. Add the sherry and broth (or water), toss in the snow peas, then cover and let steam for about 1½ minutes. Uncover, and return the pork to the pan. Mix together the sauce ingredients, and pour that into the wok. Stir-fry for a few seconds to heat and blend. Drizzle the sesame oil over, and sprinkle on optional nuts. Spoon out into a warm bowl with some rice alongside.

Variations

The possibilities are limitless. Try asparagus, sugar snap peas, young zucchini, tender bok choy, julienned broccoli stems (or broccolini), julienned carrots, scallions, hot peppers. Dried mushrooms, soaked for 30 minutes, are very tasty, as are some slivered hot peppers and fermented black beans. And, of course, you can use other meats, chicken, or seafood here.

Broiled Lamb Chop with Broiled New Potatoes

I love lamb chops, and I can't resist when I find a pair of loin chops at least 1 inch thick sitting side by side in a shrink-wrapped package at the meat counter. Expensive? Yes, and I don't really need two of them. But I give in and set aside the uneaten portion of the second one to tuck into a small casserole of French lentils. It makes an appealing second dinner.

WHAT YOU NEED

2 or 3 smallish new potatoes

Olive oil

Kosher salt

1 or 2 thick loin lamb chops

Freshly ground pepper

1 garlic clove

1 tablespoon chopped fresh
 Italian parsley

Boil the potatoes in lightly salted water for 5 minutes. Drain (don't peel), cut in half, and rub a little olive oil and salt over them. Rub salt, olive oil, and pepper over the chops, too, and arrange both the chops and the potatoes on a broiler pan. Slip them about 4 inches under a preheated broiler, and cook for 4 minutes, then turn and broil another 3 minutes. Meanwhile, make a paste of garlic and salt (see page 48) and spread it over the lamb chops after you take them out of the oven. Let rest for a minute or two while you chop some parsley. Sprinkle that over both the chops and the potatoes, and dig in. You're alone, so you can pick up the chop and nibble the meat close to the bone—it's always the best. Set aside any uneaten portions of lamb for Lamb and Lentils (recipe follows).

Variation

Cook the chops on a grill. Timing depends on how hot your fire is, so check carefully. When the flesh springs back, it is done. Or use the instant-read thermometer. Lamb shouldn't be more than 125–130° for rare.

Second Round

Lamb and Lentils

You may have one whole cooked chop that you couldn't eat, or you may have only a few bites. It doesn't matter—the meat is really just a garnish to the lentils.

WHAT YOU NEED

½ cup French green lentils

2 tablespoons chopped bacon, pancetta, or prosciutto

1 shallot, or ½ small onion, chopped

1 small garlic clove, peeled and sliced

½ rib celery, chopped, or the equivalent amount of fennel

About ¼ small jalapeño or hot red pepper, chopped

2 teaspoons light olive oil

¼ teaspoon dried thyme

⅓ bay leaf

Leftover cooked lamb, cut in small pieces

Salt

Rinse and drain the lentils. Sauté gently in a small pan the bacon, shallot, garlic, celery, and jalapeño in the olive oil for about 5 minutes, until the vegetables have softened. Add the lentils, thyme, and bay leaf, and cover by an inch with water. Bring to a boil, then turn down the heat, cover, and simmer for about 20 minutes, adding more water if necessary. Fold the lamb pieces into the lentils. Salt to taste, and cook another 5 minutes. Then supper is on the table.

About Garlic

I like to smash, peel, and chop garlic cloves rather than putting them through a press. That way you get more of the pulp along with the pungent juice. And then if you want to make a paste, simply sprinkle salt over the minced garlic, and with the flat of your large knife, smear the garlic and salt together.

Garlic has many guises: raw it is pungent; fried in hot oil it can be volatile; but slowly roasted (see page 143), or braised, garlic turns mellow and buttery.

Braised Shoulder Lamb Chops

Scott Peacock, the gifted young chef from Alabama who worked with and cared for the legendary Virginia cook Edna Lewis during her final years, once told me that one of the great lessons he learned from Edna was "the way she slowly coaxed the essence of flavor" from ingredients, be they meat, poultry, vegetables, or a combination. This slow braising of shoulder lamb chops is a good example of the technique that Scott worked out by observing her. Very little liquid is used, and by smothering the meat in a covering of parchment, then foil, and a tight-fitting lid, you make sure the juices that are "leached out" don't evaporate but fall back into the pan, penetrating the meat and vegetables. As a result, you get an intensity of flavor that is breathtaking. I have adapted their recipe here to make two servings, not only because such chops are invariably vacuum-wrapped two to a package, but because the dish is so good that I always want to use it for a second round. Every time I make it, I want to give thanks to Edna and Scott, who seemed destined to cook together to bring new life to Southern cooking.

2 shoulder lamb chops

2 teaspoons butter

1 large sweet onion, sliced fairly thick

3 fat garlic cloves, peeled and cut into slivers

Salt and freshly ground pepper

2 medium tomatoes, chopped, or 4 canned San Marzano tomatoes

¼ cup red wine

1 bay leaf

½ cup beans, such as lima or butter beans, precooked until just tender (optional)

A scattering of chopped fresh parsley

Rinse the chops and dry them thoroughly. Heat the butter in a medium skillet, and sauté the chops on both sides until well browned. Transfer the chops to a baking dish just big enough to hold them in one layer. Brown the onion slices in the skillet, scraping up the browned bits from the bottom, and after about 5 minutes, add the garlic slivers, season with salt and pepper, and cook another 5 minutes. Stir in the chopped tomatoes, and remove from the heat. Salt both sides of the chops, and season with about eight turnings of the pepper grinder. Cover the chops with the contents of the skillet, pour on the wine, and toss in the bay leaf. Cover with parchment, cut to fit, then a layer of foil and a tight-fitting cover, and put into a preheated 325° oven. After 2 hours, remove the coverings and skim off some of the fat. Stir in the beans, if using, cover again, and return to the oven for about 25 minutes. Sprinkle some parsley on top of your first serving.

NOTE For convenience, I will often prepare this dish up to the final stage of adding the beans. It's easy to skim off the fat if it has been in the refrigerator overnight, and then I'll reheat and add the beans a ½ hour before eating.

Second Rounds

You can make a delicious pasta sauce from the second chop cut into small pieces with all those delicious juices. I like to add a few sautéed mushrooms, too. Another option is to add to the chopped meat and juices a few cooked artichoke hearts along with the mushrooms, and spoon that over a serving of couscous. I like that dish liberally topped with chopped cilantro.

Moroccan-Style Lamb Shanks with Potatoes and Peas

Lamb shanks lend themselves to slow cooking, so I like to make this hearty dish-in-one on a weekend and then have it later in the week in a second incarnation. Shanks are often found two to a package in the supermarket, so it's less hassle to buy the whole package and enjoy them twice. I've adapted this recipe from Claudia Roden, who taught me always to have a jar of my own preserved lemons in the fridge to give that final spark to so many Middle Eastern and North African dishes, and I've followed her advice.

WHAT YOU NEED

2 teaspoons olive oil

1 small onion, chopped

1 fat garlic clove, peeled and slivered

1 slice fresh ginger, about the size of a 25-cent piece

⅛ teaspoon saffron threads

2 lamb shanks

Salt and freshly ground pepper

3 or 4 small new potatoes

½ cup fresh peas or frozen, defrosted

2 strips Preserved Lemon (page 241), pulp scraped off and peel julienned

3 or 4 green olives, pitted and quartered

About 1 tablespoon chopped fresh parsley and cilantro, if you have it

Heat the oil in a small heavy pot or skillet, and stir in the onion, garlic, ginger, and saffron; then lay in the lamb shanks. Cook for about 5 minutes over low heat, stirring frequently and turning the shanks over. Pour in enough water to cover, and sprinkle with about ½ teaspoon salt and several grindings of pepper. Cover, and continue to cook over low heat for 1½–2 hours, until the shanks are very tender; check the level of liquid, and add more water if necessary so that it just covers the shanks. Add the potatoes, and simmer for 20 minutes; then add the peas, preserved lemon, and olives, and cook another 4 or 5 minutes. Fish out one of the shanks and the potatoes, and place on a warm plate; then, with a fine-mesh scoop, pick up all the peas and seasonings and scatter them over the meat. Pour on some of the cooking sauce (you'll only use about half of it), and sprinkle the parsley and cilantro on top.

Variations

I've used lima beans instead of peas, as well as a handful of fava beans, when I have them in the garden; both take a little longer to cook than the peas, so allow for that. If you don't have preserved lemon, either store-bought or homemade, use a couple of slivers of fresh lemon peel, finely julienned. And don't worry if you don't have fresh cilantro—parsley alone is fine. Be sure to save the rest of the cooking sauce.

Second Round

Couscous with Lamb, Onions, and Raisins

WHAT YOU NEED

2 tablespoons raisins

1 medium onion, sliced

2 teaspoons butter

1 teaspoon olive oil

1 teaspoon honey

The meat removed from the
    leftover lamb shank, shredded

The remaining lamb-shank sauce

FOR THE COUSCOUS

½ cup couscous

Generous pinch of salt

1 teaspoon butter

1 tablespoon whole almonds,
    blanched, peeled, and lightly
    toasted

Let the raisins soak in warm water for about 20 minutes. Meanwhile, put the sliced onion in a small cooking pot with water to cover, and boil gently for about 25 minutes, until the onion is soft and the water has evaporated. Stir in the butter, olive oil, and honey, and cook another 5 minutes, until golden and caramelized. While the onion is cooking, prepare the couscous by bringing ¾ cup water to a boil in a small cooking pot and sprinkling in the couscous. Boil for 1 minute, add the salt and butter, then stir and cover. Now heat the shank meat in its cooking sauce.

When all is ready, spoon out the couscous onto a warm dinner plate, moisten it with a little of the lamb sauce, then make an indentation and spoon the meat and the rest of the sauce into it along with the honey/sweet onion/raisin mix, and scatter the almonds on top.

A Simplified Lamb Curry

For a dinner party, I often serve a roast leg of lamb, studded with garlic cloves and slathered in mustard French-style. I make sure the meat when cooked is always rosy—in fact, saignant *at the bone—and therefore good to use in any number of dishes that ordinarily call for raw lamb. And I always find myself with plenty of leftovers—one forgets how hefty a leg of lamb is these days. I wrote about some of my experiments with leftover lamb in my book* The Tenth Muse *in a section called "The Nine Lives of a Leg of Lamb." So, if you are confronted with this happy dilemma of too much lamb, you'll find nine recipes there, which can be cut down to serve one. I don't want to repeat them here, but I have since experimented with this lamb curry for one, which I find delicious.*

WHAT YOU NEED

1 tablespoon vegetable oil

1 small onion or fat shallot, chopped

¼ large bell pepper, red or green, diced

1 garlic clove, peeled and chopped

6–8 approximately ¾-inch chunks leftover roast lamb cut close to the bone, where meat is rarest

½ teaspoon fennel seeds

1½–2 tablespoons good Madras curry powder

Salt

Fresh lemon juice to taste

¾–1 cup braising liquid (any leftover pan juice, or chicken, lamb, or veal broth)

1 tablespoon shredded unsweetened coconut (optional)

½ small tart apple, peeled, seeded, and cut in slim wedges (optional)

Heat the oil in a small pan, and sauté the onion, pepper, and garlic gently for about 8 minutes, until softened. Add the lamb chunks, fennel seeds,

Lamb Curry continued

and curry powder. Salt lightly, squeeze several drops of lemon juice over, and pour on the braising liquid. Cover, and cook at a lively simmer for 10 minutes, checking to make sure your liquid isn't reducing too rapidly; if it is, add more braising liquid or water. If you are using the coconut and the apple slices, toss them into the pan for the last 5 minutes of cooking. Taste and correct seasoning, adding more salt and lemon juice as you see fit. The sauce should now be thick and coating the meat. Serve with rice or an Indian bread, and a Cucumber Raita (page 163).

Variation

If you haven't got unsweetened coconut on hand or really tart apples, use instead a small handful of raisins, in which case you may want to increase the lemon juice.

Blanquette de Veau with Leeks

This is a favorite dish of mine that I would make often when I lived in Paris in the late 1940s. I've learned to simplify it a bit and make relatively small portions. I am partial to leeks, no doubt because of my Welsh husband, who called them the poor man's asparagus, and they marry particularly well with delicate veal.

WHAT YOU NEED

1 tablespoon butter

Salt

About ¾ pound boneless veal for stew (or so the supermarket package is labeled)

All-purpose flour for dredging

1 fat shallot, sliced

A generous splash of white wine

¼ cup chicken broth

2 plump leeks

2 or 3 new potatoes or fingerlings

Herb packet of about 8 fresh parsley stems, 3 peppercorns, ½ bay leaf

½ large egg (page 112)

3 tablespoons heavy cream

2 strips Preserved Lemon (page 241), fleshy part discarded, the rind cut into

dice, or ½ teaspoon lemon juice

A sprinkling of chopped fresh parsley

Melt the butter in a medium heavy saucepan. Salt the veal pieces lightly, then dredge in flour, shaking off excess. Put them in the pan with the sizzling butter. Sauté gently over moderate heat for a few minutes, turning them until they are just lightly browned on all sides. Add the shallot slices for the last minute of sautéing. Splash in the wine, and cook down a little; then add the broth. Cover, and simmer gently for 1 hour. Cut the coarse green tops off the leeks and save for a soup. Wash the leeks carefully, cut them into 1-inch pieces, and add them to the veal along with the potatoes, peeled and cut in half, and the herb packet. Cook slowly, semi-covered, until the potatoes are tender—about 20 minutes.

Now, you can enjoy the blanquette as is, but if you want to take the time to make it velvety and soigné, here's what you do. (First remove four or five chunks of the veal, leaving in the pan just what you want for your own dinner, and store those extra pieces along with a quarter of the cooking juice.) Beat the half-egg in a small bowl until blended, then slowly add the remaining hot cooking liquid and the cream. Return this sauce to the pan with the veal, and heat it very slowly until it thickens. Sprinkle the preserved lemon and parsley on top.

Second Round

Chop the reserved veal into small pieces, and make a quick veal-sauced pasta dish.

Fresh Veal Tongue

One cold Saturday in January, I was looking for something that would be a change from the usual—something meaty that would provide good fuel and also stoke some pleasant taste memories. To my surprise, I saw a fresh veal tongue in the meat counter of the local supermarket, and I remembered that as a child I could always find a jar of Derby tongue packed in its own naturally jellied juice on our kitchen cupboard shelf. It was a standby for making a good luncheon sandwich, and I suddenly longed for just that.

First I had to prepare the tongue, because, alas, those Derby days are a thing of the past. The tongue was small, just over a pound, and it looked fresh. But since it was shrink-wrapped, I couldn't give it the smell test. I always remember Julia Child's admonition: when you get to the checkout counter, just tear off the plastic, and if your fish or meat doesn't smell impeccably fresh after you've given it a good sniff, don't pay for it. I wasn't feeling up to such a confrontation that day, but fortunately when I got the tongue home it passed muster. First I scrubbed it under running water, then I soaked it for an hour in water to cover, with a tablespoon of salt mixed in.

WHAT YOU NEED

A fresh veal tongue, about
   1 pound
1 medium onion, sliced
2 teaspoons salt

2 bay leaves
8–10 black peppercorns
3 or 4 lemon slices

After scrubbing and soaking the veal, put it in a heavy pot large enough to accommodate it, and cover it with cold water. Toss in the onion and seasonings, and bring to a boil, then lower the heat and cook at a lively simmer for 45 minutes. Let the tongue cool in the liquid until you can handle it, and peel off the tough outer skin all around. Pour off the broth through a strainer and save it. Now for the final braising with this vegetable accompaniment:

2 tablespoons butter	celery root, peeled and cut in
1 medium onion, cut into chunks	chunks (optional)
3 or 4 slim carrots, peeled and	2 or 3 small new potatoes, cut in
cut into sections	half
A root vegetable, such as a	A splash of Madeira
turnip, a parsnip, or part of a	

Melt the butter in the pot in which you are cooking the tongue, and sauté the vegetables for a minute or so. Add the Madeira, let it cook down a little, and lay the tongue on top. Pour about ¾ cup of the tongue cooking liquid around it, cover with foil and then with the pot's cover, and set it all in a preheated 325° oven for 1 hour, checking once to see that there is sufficient liquid, and adding more tongue broth if necessary. The veggies should be moist but not swimming in liquid. When it's done, cut yourself three or four diagonal slices, and spread them on a warm plate surrounded by the vegetables.

Second Round

Try a tongue sandwich with lettuce, mayonnaise, and Dijon mustard, with a couple of cornichons alongside.

Third Round

Warm slightly any remaining slices of tongue, and serve in a warm Sauce Gribiche (page 160).

A Small Meatloaf with a French Accent

Recently I stumbled upon a package in the meat counter of my nearby super-market that contained ⅓ pound each of ground beef, pork, and veal—just enough to make a small meatloaf for two, or for one with some welcome left-overs. I was elated, not only because I wanted to make a small meatloaf and I'd found it so hard to get the mix that I needed in modest amounts, but also because I felt it was a sign of the times. Maybe supermarkets are finally waking up to the fact that so many New Yorkers live alone and should be catered to, instead of forcing us to buy more than we need. So I took the package home and made myself this meatloaf, sneaking in a few French flavors to jazz it up a bit.

WHAT YOU NEED

⅓ pound ground beef

⅓ pound ground pork

⅓ pound ground veal

2 plump garlic cloves

1 teaspoon salt, or more as
    needed

2 shallots, or 1 small onion

4 or 5 sprigs fresh parsley,
    preferably flat-leaved

1 teaspoon dried porcini (no
    soaking needed)

¼ teaspoon *herbes de Provence*

¼ cup red or white wine

Freshly ground pepper

½ bay leaf

1 strip bacon

VEGETABLE ACCOMPANIMENTS

Olive oil

Salt

2 new potatoes, cut in eighths
    lengthwise

2 young carrots, peeled

1 young parsnip, peeled and cut
    in half lengthwise, or another
    root vegetable similarly
    prepared

The night before you're planning to have a meatloaf dinner, put the meats in a bowl. Smash the garlic cloves, peel and chop them fine, then, with the flat of your chef's knife, mash them into a paste with ¼ teaspoon of the salt. Chop the shallots and parsley, and crumble the porcini. Add all these seasonings to the meats, along with the *herbes de Provence,* the wine, several grindings of your pepper mill, and the remaining salt. Mix thoroughly with your hands, squishing the meat with your fingers. When thoroughly mixed, cover the bowl with plastic wrap and let macerate for 24 hours in the refrigerator.

The next day, remove the meat from the fridge and pull off a tiny piece. Cook it quickly in a small skillet, then taste it to see if it needs more seasoning. If so, add whatever is needed. Form the meat into a small loaf. Break the bay leaf into three pieces, and arrange them on top of the loaf; then lay the bacon strip, also cut in thirds, on top. Transfer the loaf to a medium baking pan. Rub a little olive oil and salt over the vegetables you want as an accompaniment, and distribute them around the meatloaf. Bake in a preheated 350° oven for 45–50 minutes, turning the vegetables once.

Everything is done when the meat looks lightly browned, the bacon a bit crisp, and the veggies tender (the internal temperature of the loaf should be about 150°). Let rest for at least 5 minutes, then cut three or more slices, and arrange on a warm plate, with the vegetables surrounding the meat and the juice poured over.

Second Round

Leftover meatloaf is good cold—but not overly chilled. Eaten with a dab of Dijon mustard, little cornichons, and a glass of red wine, it will taste almost like a French country pâté.

A Slice of Baked Ham

We used to get as a Christmas present from James Beard a whole genuine Southern ham, and it sustained us throughout the winter months. But it's not so easy for the person living alone to cope with that much ham. My solution is to buy about a 1-pound slice of ham and bake it. I can enjoy it in this old family recipe, which gets rid of the usual watery, oversalted taste that most of our commercial hams have today and gives the meat a wonderful flavor. You can have a few good slices of it the first night for dinner, and the leftovers are there to be used in all kinds of ways.

WHAT YOU NEED

1 slice ham, about 1 pound*
About 1 tablespoon Dijon
    mustard
Milk (up to 1 cup)

3 or 4 fresh sage leaves, if
    available, or 3 dried, or a
    sprinkling of dried rosemary
2–3 teaspoons dark-brown sugar

---

*Ideally, you want a slice that is at least 1 inch thick, but that is hard to find, so I often settle for the supermarket slice, which is about ½ inch. If you find a butcher who will cut you the thicker slice, by all means take it. It will probably be a good 2 pounds, but you can use the ham in so many ways, it will serve you well.

Put the ham in a shallow baking dish that will just accommodate the slice, and smear the mustard on top. Pour milk all around, enough to almost cover the surface, lay the sage leaves on top, and sprinkle the sugar over it. Bake in a preheated 350° oven for 1 hour, occasionally opening the oven and spooning some of the curdling milk over the top.

Your first portion of this will taste particularly good with a purée of parsnips (or another root vegetable) mixed with potatoes alongside.

There are many, many suggestions for using the rest of the ham through-out these pages.

FISH AND SEAFOOD

Try to be a little adventurous in buying fresh fish. It isn't so easy if you don't live close to a good fish market. But more and more supermarkets that promote fresh foods are catering to the single cook and offer a fish fillet or steak in a single portion.

Farm-Raised Snapper with Fennel, Scallions, and Red Pepper

I recently saw something labeled "Snapper Lake Victoria (Kenya) Farm Raised," and it looked glistening and fresh through its plastic wrap. Because the slice, just under a pound, was rather plump and not firm-fleshed and fatty, I felt it would take well to braising with some vegetables. I happened to have about half of a small fennel in the vegetable bin, and some roasted red peppers (from a jar, another good standby item, or put away your own [see page 242]), so I decided to make a bed of those aromatics and, when they were cooked semi-soft, to tuck the fish in and let everything finish cooking together. It was particularly delicious with leftover cooked potatoes browned in duck fat.

WHAT YOU NEED

½ small fennel bulb (reserve leaves)	3 or 4 fairly wide strips roasted red pepper
1 tablespoon olive oil	¼ cup white wine
Salt and freshly ground pepper	3 black Mediterranean olives, pitted and roughly cut
1 thick slice snapper, ½–¾ pound	A sprinkling of chopped fresh parsley and fennel leaves
2 scallions, chopped	
Large pinch of *herbes de Provence*	

Slice the fennel very thin. If you have a mandoline, that will do the job well. Heat the oil in a small frying pan, and scatter the fennel pieces in. Salt and pepper lightly, and cook over very low heat; if the fennel seems to be browning and drying out, add a little water. When it begins to soften, after about 5 minutes, clear the bottom of the pan and lay in the snapper, salted and peppered lightly. Sprinkle on the scallions, the *herbes de Provence,* and scatter the red pepper on top. Pour in the wine, and braise for 5–6 minutes, covered, turning once, and adding the olives during the last minute of cooking. Garnish with chopped parsley and fennel leaves.

Second Round

If your eyes were bigger than your tummy, which often happens to me, retrieve a piece of the fish, preferably a thinner, side piece that cooks faster, and make this fish salad: Cut the cooked fish into bite-sized pieces, and dress it with Winter Green Sauce (page 159). Surround it with some cucumbers and tomatoes and more olives, as well as a hard-boiled egg and some tart greens, for a most satisfying lunch.

Baked Bass with Fingerlings and Zucchini

This is a nice dish for summer, when zucchini is abundant and the fingerlings are delicate.

WHAT YOU NEED

A whole bass, 1¼–1½ pounds
Salt
Olive oil
3 or 4 small fingerling potatoes
1 small-to-medium zucchini
Freshly ground pepper

2 scallions, chopped
2 tablespoons chopped fresh
   parsley mixed with other fresh
   herbs, such as dill or tarragon
Juice of 1 lemon

Preheat the oven to 400°.

Rinse and dry the fish, and rub some salt and olive oil over it. Peel the fingerlings, and cut lengthwise into quarters. Cut the zucchini in half lengthwise, and then into 1½-inch pieces. Toss the potatoes and zucchini in a little olive oil, and salt and pepper them lightly. Spread them out on the bottom of an oval baking dish big enough to hold the fish. Fill the cavity of the bass with the scallions and herbs, sprinkle a little lemon juice and salt over it, and lay the fish on top of the vegetables. Bake for 25–30 minutes, or until the flesh of the bass is opaque.

Second Round Suggestions

You're bound to have some leftover fish, so make some Fish Cakes (page 68) later in the week, or use the fish in a summery salad (see page 157).

Fillet of Fish in Parchment

Making a parchment envelope in which to steam a fillet of fish surrounded by aromatic vegetables may sound a bit fancy for just one, but cooking in parchment is actually one of the simplest and most effective ways of steaming, because it seals in the flavors. What a treat it is to have that golden-tinged, puffed-up half-moon of parchment on your plate, and then to tear it open and breathe in all the heady aromas. Moreover, you'll have no cleanup afterward; just wipe off the Silpat mat and throw away the parchment after you've scraped and scooped up every last delicious morsel and its jus.

If you want just one meal out of this, get about a 6-ounce fillet of flounder, halibut, salmon, red snapper—whatever looks good. Or, as I did recently, try tilapia, which is quite readily available these days and at a reasonable price. But I bought almost twice the amount I needed, so I could play with the other half of the cooked fillet a couple of days later.

I learned from Katy Sparks, whose book, Sparks in the Kitchen, *is full of great cooking tips from a chef to the home cook, the trick of pre-roasting several slices of new potato so they can go in the parchment package. This way you have a complete, balanced meal-in-one cooked all together.*

WHAT YOU NEED

Olive oil

2 or 3 smallish new potatoes, cut into ½-inch slices

Salt and freshly ground pepper

6-ounce fillet of flounder, halibut, tilapia, salmon, or red snapper, or more if you want leftovers

About ⅓ medium zucchini, cut into julienne strips

½ medium carrot, peeled and cut into very thin julienne strips

1 scallion, white and tender green, cut into lengthwise strips

3 slices fresh ginger approximately the size of 25-cent pieces, peeled and cut into julienne strips

A splash of white wine

A sprinkling of fresh herbs, if available (such as parsley, chives, tarragon, or summer savory)

Preheat the oven to 425°.

Oil lightly the center of your Silpat mat set on a baking sheet, or, if you don't have the mat, oil a piece of foil. Scatter the potato slices over the oiled area, then turn them. Salt and pepper lightly. Roast in the preheated oven for 10 minutes, turning once.

Meanwhile, cut off an 18-inch piece of parchment paper, and fold it in half. Open it up, and on one half place the fish alongside the folded edge, after salting and peppering it on both sides (see illustrations on preceding page and opposite). Pile the zucchini, carrot, scallion, and ginger on top of the fish, salt again lightly, and splash on enough wine to bathe the fillet(s) lightly. After the potato slices have had their 10-minute pre-roasting, arrange them on top or around the edge of the fish and sprinkle the herbs over all. Fold the other half of the parchment over, then fold in the open edge twice, and pleat it all around to make a semicircular airtight package. If it tends to open up where the folded edges meet, secure that place with a binder clip or a large paper clip. Place on the sheet pan, and bake for 12 minutes. If you have a fairly thick fillet, you may need to bake it 1 or

2 minutes more. Test with a skewer; if it goes in easily, the fish is done. Plunk the whole parchment package on a big dinner plate, and enjoy.

NOTE If you deliberately cooked more fish than you need, remove what you won't want the first time around, and save it for a second round.

Second Round

You can make a delicious salad with the remaining fish. Arrange a bed of watercress or young arugula leaves on a salad plate, and set the fish on top. Spoon 2 or 3 tablespoons of Sauce Gribiche over it (see page 160), or, if you don't have that handy, use about 2 tablespoons mayonnaise thinned and tarted up with a little plain yogurt or lemon juice and seasoned with a small, finely chopped cornichon (or part of a dill pickle) and ½ teaspoon capers. Garnish with some strips of roasted red pepper— your own (see page 242) or from a jar—a few black olives, and some cherry tomatoes. Or try the Fish Salad recipe on page 157. These are just suggestions. Use your imagination, based on what you may have on hand.

Fish Cakes

Those little bits of fish that you didn't finish, or that you purposely put aside for another meal, take on new life in these scrumptious fish cakes. My rule of thumb is to use equal parts cooked fish and potatoes. If the fish you are using has been fried, scrape off the crusty exterior, because you want the cakes to be smooth inside.

⅔–¾ cup flaked cooked fish

⅔–¾ cup mashed cooked
potatoes

1 or 2 scallions, including tender
green, chopped fine

Grated fresh ginger to taste

Salt and freshly ground pepper to
taste

Butter and/or light olive oil for
frying

Mix the fish and the potatoes with a fork, then work in the other ingredients. You'll probably want to start with about ¼ teaspoon of the grated ginger, which really lifts the flavors, but use more if you want. Form the mixture into two round patties. Heat a tablespoon of butter or oil (I always prefer a mixture of both, so the butter won't burn), and when it is sizzling, lay in the fish cakes and cook over medium heat for about 4 minutes on each side.

Variations

Vary the seasonings. Sorrel is particularly good with salmon, but you would need to sauté a small handful of leaves first, gently, in a little butter, until they turned limp and gray-green in color, then chop them and mix in with the fish and potatoes. Fresh tarragon, chives, and dill also make good complements. And if you want your fish cakes very crusty, brush them with beaten egg and dredge them in panko, those wonderful Japanese breadcrumbs that give such a crusty finish.

Sautéed Shrimp

I make this simple shrimp dish often, but only recently did I discover how good it is served on a bed of farro (see page 190), which Lidia Bastianich introduced me to. It's also delicious with rice, grits, or polenta. You'll get a good two meals out of this amount.

WHAT YOU NEED

About 10 ounces medium shrimp

2 tablespoons light olive oil

1 fat garlic clove, peeled and sliced thin

Salt and freshly ground pepper

A splash of white wine or dry vermouth

A scattering of chopped fresh parsley (or basil or tarragon if you have some)

Peel the shrimp, leaving the tail intact if you like picking them up and sucking the meat out of the tail end. Remove any black digestive tracts. Heat the oil in a wok or a heavy sauté pan, scatter in the garlic, and toss the slices in the hot oil for about 1 minute without browning them; then add the shrimp, season with salt and pepper, and stir-fry for about 2 minutes, until the flesh has turned opaque and rosy. Splash in the wine, cook down slightly, scatter parsley and/or other herbs on top, and they're ready to go.

Variation

To make a more substantial dish, scatter in several mushrooms (halved if big), and stir-fry with the garlic for 2 or 3 minutes. When you add the shrimp, toss in about ¼ cup frozen peas or a small handful of pea pods or sugar snaps and a couple of scallions, sliced lengthwise. Chunks of asparagus are good, too, when in season.

Second Round

A nice shrimp salad is always good. You can also reheat the shrimp and add either fresh ripe chopped tomatoes or a canned tomato squeezed with a little of its juice, to make a sauce for pasta. Recently I had a small treasure trove of cooked shrimp, and I cooked some thin-sliced fennel in a bit of olive oil and water until tender, then added about six shrimp, and had this over some fast-cooking polenta for a very quick supper.

Pan-Seared Salmon

Salmon is probably the fish that Americans cook most often. It is readily available, quick to prepare, and can be dressed in many different ways. I always buy a bigger portion than I need, so I have some for the next day. I find searing the fillet in a hot skillet on both sides, and then letting it finish in the oven briefly, is a good way to keep the salmon tasty on the outside and moist inside.

WHAT YOU NEED

Light olive oil
Kosher salt and freshly ground
    pepper

8–10 ounces salmon fillet
Garnish: lemon wedge and
    butter, or pesto

Rub a little olive oil and salt and pepper on both sides of the salmon. Heat a medium heavy skillet until almost smoking, and lay in the fillet, skin side down. Sear over high heat about 2 minutes, then turn and sear the other side 1½ minutes. Put the skillet in a preheated 350° oven, and let finish cooking for about 5 minutes. Test by cutting into a piece to see if it is done to your liking. Dress the salmon with a little butter and lemon juice or a small spoonful of pesto over the portion you are going to eat. I particularly like salmon with roasted asparagus dressed with a sesame vinaigrette (see page 149), so some of those Asian flavors seep into the fish.

Second Rounds

You can use the leftover salmon in so many ways—in a corn pancake (page 130), a salad or a sandwich, a rice dish, British Kedgeree (page 174), or perhaps a New England Bouillabaisse (page 91).

Broiled Bluefish or Mackerel over a Bed of Artichoke Hearts and Potatoes

Bluefish and mackerel are both rather fatty fish, and they take well to broiling, particularly when the fillet sits on a bed of flavorful vegetables and they exchange flavors. I also like this preparation because it requires only one pan. If it's a handsome fireproof baking dish, it can come right to the table. Otherwise, scoop everything up with a spatula and serve on a warm plate.

WHAT YOU NEED

2 teaspoons olive oil

½ medium onion, sliced

2 or 3 new potatoes

About 8 artichoke hearts, frozen
    or fresh

Salt

1 small or ½ medium tomato,
    chopped

10–13-ounce bluefish or mackerel
    fillet

Freshly ground pepper

A sprinkling of chopped fresh
    parsley and dill or tarragon, if
    available (otherwise, a pinch
    of dried)

A lemon wedge

Heat the oil in a skillet or a heatproof baking dish large enough to hold the fillet (it can be cut in two pieces). Toss the onion into the pan, and sauté for 2–3 minutes; then add the potatoes. Pour in about ½ cup water, and let simmer, covered, for 15 minutes, checking to be sure there is just a little water. Add the frozen or fresh artichoke hearts, and simmer, covered, for 5 minutes, or until they are almost tender. Sprinkle on some salt, and add the chopped tomato. Let cook just until the the tomato has released its liquid. Remove from the heat. Rub the fish fillet with salt and pepper, and lay it, in two pieces if necessary, on top of the vegetables. Set the pan or dish about 3 inches under the broiler, and broil for 8–10 minutes, depending on the thickness of the fillet. Test with a fork after 8 minutes; the flesh should not be resistant. Save a portion of the fish for a second round, and sprinkle the herbs over what you are about to eat, served with a wedge of lemon alongside.

Second Round

This is another fish that takes well to a salad (see pages 62 and 68).

Roasted Branzino (Loup de Mer)

When I spotted this appealing whole fish at Citarella, just about a pound, I thought that it would take well to roasting, and it did. I love to tackle a whole fish by myself because it is such pleasantly messy work. I made sure the fishmonger left the head on when it was gutted and scaled, because I wanted to relish the cheeks, as Irene Kuo's husband taught me to do when we went out for a Chinese dinner to celebrate the publication of her book, The Key to Chinese Cooking. *He carefully plucked out the cheeks with his chopsticks and offered them to me ceremoniously.*

WHAT YOU NEED

Olive oil

Salt

1 whole branzino, gutted and
    scaled

A handful of fresh cilantro leaves

3 or 4 scallions, trimmed

1 or 2 slivers small fresh hot
    pepper, such as jalapeño

½ lemon

Rub a little olive oil and salt over the fish. Stuff the cavity with the cilantro, trimmed whole scallions, and fresh hot pepper. Cut three slices of lemon very thin, halve them, and scatter the pieces over the top of the fish. Roast in a preheated 425° oven for 25 minutes. Serve with a wedge of lemon (incidentally, the thin lemon strips roasted on top of the fish are to be eaten; I find them delectable). A potato dish, such as the one for Julia (page 135), goes well with this, as would a vegetable roasted alongside.

Second Round

If you don't finish all the fish, what's left over would taste good in British Kedgeree (page 174).

I love mussels, and I like to cook up a couple of pounds, so that after an initial meal of feasting on them, I'll have plenty left to dress up in different ways. Ed Giobbi pointed out to me that less than sixty years ago these sweet, briny mollusks were considered trash fish in New England, and that the only Americans who appreciated them were first-generation Italians and Portuguese. I certainly never encountered mussels until I went to France in my mid-twenties.

When Ed was working on his book *Pleasures of the Good Earth,* I urged him to include his story about mussel-hunting when he was a boy. This is what he wrote:

> During the Depression, my father, my godfather, Tomasso, and his father and their friends would drive to New Haven, Connecticut, to gather mussels. They gathered mussels most of the year, and they gathered them by the bushel, bringing them home tied securely on the running board of the Model T Ford one of them owned. My father used to take me with him and I remember all the wonderful discoveries I made while gathering mussels. The fascinating tidal pools teeming with life, the snails, the starfish, and an occasional horseshoe crab—it was worlds apart from the drab factory town we lived in. The women would wait for our return. Then they would wash the mussels, laughing and gossiping all the while—and prepare the sauces and stuffing for them. The men would deftly open the mussels with their pocketknives (and they all had pocketknives) as they drank my father's wine, smoked Italian cigars, and chatted about their gardens or their own wine.
>
> I suppose I remember these occasions because they were joyous, and I tend to think of the Depression with some nostalgia. The gathering and preparing of the food was a group effort and everyone was loving and open. Perhaps that's why I have a special reverence for food.

Today mussels have become so appreciated that they are cultivated all over, and often what we get are fleshier and even more succulent than the wild variety. They also have less beard and less grit, which makes them easier to clean.

Steamed Mussels

Steamed mussels make a lovely dish to eat alone slowly, plucking the plump flesh from the shells as messily as you like and sopping up the heavenly liquor with chunks of French bread.

WHAT YOU NEED

2 pounds mussels	¾ cup white wine
2 fat shallots	Chopped fresh parsley

Wash all the mussels, and scrub them if they seem at all gritty. Scrape away any beard. Chop up the shallots, toss them into a large heavy pot, and pour in the wine. Bring to a boil and simmer for 2 minutes, to reduce the wine slightly, then dump in all the mussels. Cover the pot, and cook over brisk heat until all the shells have opened (if any have remained firmly shut after the rest have opened, discard them). Dish up into a warm bowl as many mussels as your healthy appetite dictates, scatter a small handful of chopped parsley over them, and spoon most of the liquid on top.

Shell the remaining mussels, and pack them and the broth tightly in a refrigerator container, reserving about a dozen handsome shells.

Second Round

CHINESE STYLE

I got the idea for these seasonings out of Ken Hom's engaging book *Easy Family Recipes from a Chinese-American Childhood.* He remembers how his family enjoyed this treat, using chopsticks and accompanying the mussels with a bowl of rice. So, if you want to do the same, get the rice going first (see page 169). Pour the liquid from the remaining mussels into a small pot; you'll want about ½ cup; if you haven't enough add some light chicken broth to make it up. Cut a medium clove of garlic into slivers, and scatter them into the liquid. Grate some fresh ginger—about ½ teaspoon—directly into the pot, stir in ½ teaspoon good curry powder, a splash of dry sherry, 2 teaspoons soy sauce, and a generous pinch of sugar. Bring to a gentle boil and simmer for a few minutes, then fold in most of the remaining mussels (you want to reserve eight to twelve, depending on their size, for the third round). Simmer just long enough to heat the mussels, then spoon them over a serving of warm rice. Sprinkle on a chopped scallion and a tablespoon or so of chopped cilantro or parsley.

Third Rounds

ON THE HALF SHELL WITH DRESSING

I like to have the remaining mussels bathed in a chilled sauce and returned to their shells. It makes a nice offering if someone stops by for a drink, or just to enjoy alone. Prepare a vinaigrette with 2 teaspoons red-wine vinegar, a large pinch of salt, and 2 tablespoons olive oil. Add about ¼ red pepper cut into small dice, 2 chopped scallions, ½ hard-boiled egg, chopped, and a couple of tablespoons chopped parsley (if you have some tarragon, that's good, too). Marinate the reserved mussels in this sauce for an hour or so, or even overnight. Spoon the mussels into the reserved shells; you may want to use two mussels, if they are very small, per shell. Drizzle the remaining vinaigrette over them. Eat by just sucking the mussel from the shell into your mouth.

À L'ESCARGOT

Sometimes I prefer my mussels in the shell warm instead of chilled. Recently I noticed them on a bistro menu in Paris served in escargot butter, and I ordered them. They came on an escargot plate, swimming in heady garlic butter, and they were scrumptious—better than snails usually are. So, of course, I've been doing them that way *chez moi* ever since.

For the escargot butter: Mash 2 tablespoons butter with 1 fat clove of garlic and 1 shallot, both finely minced, then dried by squeezing them in a towel. Add pepper to taste, and work in about 1 tablespoon chopped fresh parsley. Then all you need do is tuck one or two mussels, depending on their size, into the indentation in the escargot plate, and top it with about ½ teaspoon of the snail butter. Fill up as much of the snail plate as you like, and pop into a 400° oven, cooking until the contents are hot and bubbling—about 5 minutes. If you have any leftover snail butter, it's good on any kind of fish or seafood, and even vegetables. Make double the quantity the next time if you find it's something you want to have handy. You can freeze it, too.

Two Soups for All Seasons

A good soup can make a meal. Soup is a great catchall for the many bits of leftover vegetables, meat juices, trimmings, even the rind left from a wedge of Parmesan that has been devoured. Americans tend to be profligate because of the abundance in this land of plenty, but in most other parts of the world good cooks are born thrifty and are proud of making something out of nothing. I remember how Jacques Pépin, when he was working with Julia on their PBS series, was rather scornful of how all the trimmings were going to waste. He said that in his kitchen he always had a big empty milk carton at hand, and into it would go all the peelings and tough stems and end pieces; then he'd put it in the freezer. When it was full and he wanted to make a soup, he'd pull out the carton, slash it open, and dump all those discards into his soup pot. Not a bad idea for the lone cook, particularly in these days of soaring food prices.

Chicken Stock or Broth

Don't throw away your chicken carcass or the package of giblets. Here's a way of making a simple chicken stock (or broth—I use the terms interchangeably) that you'll be using in all kinds of soups. This will produce only about 4 cups, so you may want to freeze the chicken elements until you have enough to make at least twice that amount.

WHAT YOU NEED

Chicken carcass*

A packet of giblets, heart, and
    neck of a chicken

1 onion, quartered

1 small carrot

1 rib celery

Several fresh parsley stems

Salt

*Preferably uncooked, but if you have only a cooked carcass, by all means use it, as long as you add some fresh uncooked parts, such as extra giblets and neck, and maybe one or two wings.

Put the chicken carcass, the neck, and the packet of giblets (but not the liver) in a big pot with the vegetables and parsley, and cover with cold water. Bring to a boil, skim off any foam, then reduce the heat and cook at a lively simmer, semi-covered, for at least an hour, or longer if you want a more intense flavor. Season with only about ½ teaspoon salt halfway through cooking; you don't want it too salty, in case it is going to be reduced later in a soup or a sauce. Strain the stock, cool, and pour into whatever size containers you wish. You can refrigerate for 4 or 5 days and freeze for up to about 6 months.

Beef Stock

On page 35, I describe making a Beef Shank and Oxtail Ragù so that I can benefit from the rich broth it yields. That's the best way I know of making a good beef stock, and you get the benefit of several good meals. So if you see oxtails on special in your supermarket, or some shank meat, by all means snatch up either of them and use the same aromatics to make a stock you can store in the freezer.

Storing Stock in Ice Trays

This is a useful trick, particularly for anyone cooking in small quantities. Pour some of the cooled stock into an ice tray and freeze. When frozen solid, remove the cubes of stock and put them in small freezer bags. This way you can easily retrieve a few cubes, or even just one, when you need a small amount to make a pan sauce or to thin and flavor a sauce or a soup.

Substitutes for Homemade Stocks

I like to make my own broths and stocks when I can. I enjoy putting to good use bones and carcasses, giblets, and vegetable trimmings, knowing that I am going to have a delicious, pure, meaty soup to use in all sorts of ways. It doesn't really take much time, but you do have to be around while the soup perks away on the stove. Of course, there will be many occasions when your own supply is low and you'll have to rely on what the super-market offers. Fortunately, today you can get good low-sodium chicken and beef broth in a can or a plastic container, and clam juice that just needs diluting (half water/half clam juice—and don't add any salt) to use for fish stock. These make perfectly acceptable substitutes, and what you don't use up immediately can be frozen in ice trays (see facing page) for easy access.

In more sophisticated markets, you may find frozen *glace de viande,* which is essentially well-seasoned meat or duck stock that has been greatly reduced until almost syrupy, and that is well worth having in your freezer. You need just a bit—about ½ teaspoon, chipped off the frozen block—added to a pan sauce for one. It will turn it into something special.

A Basic Vegetable Soup

Here's a master recipe for a vegetable soup that you can make just for yourself when you have the urge, on a cold day, or when garden greens are in abundance in the summer.

WHAT YOU NEED

2 teaspoons butter, plus more as optional finish

1 smallish onion, peeled and chopped

1 smallish new potato, peeled and chopped, or more if needed

2½ cups chicken stock (page 81) or water or a combination

A large handful of greens (spinach, Swiss chard, beet greens, turnip greens), tough stems removed, shredded

Salt and freshly ground pepper

About 1 tablespoon heavy cream (optional)

Melt the butter in a 1-quart pot, and sauté the onion gently for a few minutes. Add the potato, sweat that with the onion another minute, then pour the stock or water over it. Bring to a boil, reduce the heat, and simmer, partially covered, for about 25 minutes, until the potato is very soft. Stir in the greens; spinach will take less than 5 minutes, other greens may need longer, depending on how young they are. Taste and determine for yourself. At this point, add just enough salt to your liking and a few grindings of the pepper mill. You may need more liquid if it has cooked down too rapidly. Serve as is, or mash it up a little with a potato masher or a fork. If you want a really smooth soup, spin everything in the food processor, put it through a vegetable mill, or use an immersion blender. Reheat if necessary, pour into a bowl, and swirl a little butter or cream on top.

Variations

The possibilities are limitless. Here are a few suggestions:

1. For nonleafy vegetables, such as zucchini, asparagus, peas, string beans, broccoli, and carrots, eliminate the potato and sauté the vegetable you're using along with the onion. If you decide to purée the soup when cooked, you might want to add 3–4 tablespoons of heavy cream.

2. To create a more substantial soup that can make a meal, top your bowl with one or two croutons, and grate some Parmesan or other aged cheese on top. You might also garnish with some slivers of ham or dried sausage or any leftover meat, shredded.

3. Use about ¼ cup cooked dried beans instead of the potato (canned are fine as long as you drain and rinse them to get rid of the canned taste of the liquid).

4. Thicken the soup with 3 or 4 tablespoons of white sauce or cooked rice, and purée.

5. Swirl some heavy cream on top, and scatter some fresh herbs over it—marjoram, tarragon, dill, chives, and basil are all good.

Leek and Potato Soup

This is really another take on the preceding vegetable soup, but it differs enough in detail to warrant a full-dress recipe. It is without question one of my favorite soups, and I usually plant a couple of rows of leeks in my garden so I can indulge myself at a moment's notice. This is one soup in which I prefer to use water rather than stock, so that nothing interferes with the sweet, pronounced flavor of the leeks.

WHAT YOU NEED

1 big, fat leek, or 2 slightly slimmer ones

1 smallish onion

2 small-to-medium new potatoes

1 tablespoon butter

3 cups water, or more as needed

Salt

Freshly ground pepper

1–2 tablespoons heavy cream (optional)

Trim the leek(s), discarding the tough green tops, and cut them into 1-inch chunks. Rinse them thoroughly, and drain. Peel and chop the onion and potatoes. Melt the butter in a medium heavy pot, and sauté the onion for a few minutes, then add the leeks and potatoes, and sweat them over low heat another few minutes, stirring frequently. Pour in the water, add a pinch of salt, and bring to a boil. Cook at a lively simmer, with cover askew, for 1 hour, until the potatoes are velvety soft. Now mash roughly with a potato masher or a slotted spoon, and add considerably more salt to taste, and a few grindings of the pepper mill. Serve as is, or swirl some cream on top.

Variation

For a creamier soup, purée everything with an immersion blender or in a food processor, and swirl in additional cream. Either enjoy hot, or turn it into a vichyssoise by adding at least ¼ cup cream and sprinkling chives on top. If you want it both hot and cold, prepare double the amount, and put away half for a later treat of vichyssoise.

SORREL SOUP

In summer you may find sorrel in farmers' markets or, if possible, grow some in your garden. Then you can easily make a simple version of that delicious French soup *Potage Germiny* by adding 1 cup of sorrel leaves, washed, stemmed, and cut in strips, to the leek, onions, and potatoes after you have sweated them. Finish the soup by puréeing and adding cream as described above.

Mushroom Soup

Here is a quick way to make a delicious, intensely flavored mushroom soup that isn't too rich, because it is thickened with cooked rice rather than cream.

WHAT YOU NEED

About 1 tablespoon dried porcini and/or other dried mushroom

1 tablespoon butter

1 small shallot (or ½ large one), chopped fine

4 medium fresh mushrooms, roughly chopped

Salt

1 cup or more chicken stock (page 81), or part stock and part water

¼ cup cooked rice

A scattering of chopped fresh parsley and/or chives and tarragon

Soak the dried mushroom in ¼ cup warm water for 20 minutes.

Melt the butter in a small pot, and sauté the shallot gently for a minute. Add the fresh mushrooms and the dried, squeezing out the draining water (save it). Sprinkle a little salt on top, and sauté, stirring now and then, for a few minutes. Pour in the chicken stock, the mushroom soaking liquid, and the rice, and cook gently for 10 minutes. Taste, and correct the seasoning. Purée in a food processor or blender or use an immersion blender until you have a relatively smooth soup. Pour into a warm bowl, and sprinkle fresh herbs on top.

Pumpkin or Winter Squash Soup

This is a good way to use that extra pumpkin or squash you may have roasted. It makes an unusually pleasing soup.

WHAT YOU NEED

1 tablespoon butter

1 medium onion, chopped fine

About 2 cups roasted pumpkin or winter-squash chunks (see page 144)

2 cups light chicken stock

¼ teaspoon grated fresh ginger

Salt

1 tablespoon heavy cream, or more as needed

A small fresh grating of nutmeg

Melt the butter in a small heavy pot, and sauté the onion gently for 5 minutes. Add the pumpkin or squash and stock, and simmer for 30 minutes. Mash the pumpkin or squash right in the soup, using a fork or a potato masher, or, if you prefer a smoother texture, purée the soup with an immersion blender or in a food processor. Stir in the ginger, turn the soup into a warm soup bowl, and spoon the cream over it, with a sprinkling of nutmeg on top.

Avgolemono Soup

If you've tasted a well-made avgolemono with its velvety texture and lemony flavor, you'll long to make it at home. And it's so simple, particularly if you've just boned a chicken breast and have the rib cage handy, or if you have some chicken broth in your freezer.

WHAT YOU NEED

Chicken bones, such as the ribs and back, and/or neck and giblets, or 1 cup chicken stock
1 small chopped onion and several fresh parsley stems, if you're making the stock from scratch
1 egg, beaten
Salt
½ lemon

GARNISH

A few strips or small chunks leftover cooked chicken breast
A scattering of chopped fresh parsley leaves

Put the chicken bones and giblets, if using, in a small pot along with the onion and parsley stems, and cover with 1¾ cups water. Bring to a boil, then simmer, covered, for about 30 minutes; you should now have about 1 cup of broth. With a slotted spoon, fish out the parsley stems, onion pieces, chicken bones, and giblets, and discard. (If you're using ready-made stock instead, just bring a cup of it to a boil.) Toward the end of the cooking time, scoop up ¼ cup of broth and pour slowly into the beaten egg as you whisk steadily. Pour this tempered egg back into the broth, continuing to whisk over very low heat until lightly thickened. Season the soup with salt and several squeezes of the lemon. Taste, and determine how much you want; it should be quite lemony. Scatter in the cooked chicken, and let warm through; then top your bowl of this blissful soup with a little chopped parsley.

Lobster Bisque

This is a rich, comforting soup to make if you have treated yourself to a whole steamed lobster (see page 254). You should have about 2 cups of lobster broth left in your pot after steaming, so be sure to save it. Also, check and scrape out any bits of lobster flesh still lodged in the shells, and use them as a garnish.

WHAT YOU NEED

1 tablespoon butter

1 medium-small onion, chopped

½ rib celery, chopped

1 medium-small new potato, peeled and cut into dice

2 or 3 fresh parsley stems

2 cups lobster broth (see headnote)

¼ cup cooked rice*

Salt and freshly ground pepper

¼ cup heavy cream

Chopped parsley or chives

*The rice is used here as a light thickening agent for the soup. If you don't have some cooked rice handy, instead you can work in 2 teaspoons soft butter mixed with 2 teaspoons flour, and swirl that into the warm soup.

Melt the butter in a small pot, and stir in the onion and celery. Cook gently for a few minutes, then add the potato, parsley stems, and lobster broth. Simmer for about 20 minutes, until the potato is tender. Remove a ladleful of the broth, and spin in a food processor or a blender with the rice until smooth. Stir this thickener into the soup, salt lightly (remembering that the lobster broth is salty), and add a few turns of the pepper mill. Remove the parsley stems, stir in any lobster bits along with the heavy cream, and heat through. Serve in a warm bowl, and sprinkle chopped fresh parsley leaves and/or chives on top.

A New England Bouillabaisse

This mock bouillabaisse is so scrumptious that you would never know it had anything "left over" in it. You do have to stop and pick up a dozen or so fresh mussels and a few clams the day you're making it, but otherwise everything else is at hand, and you can put this together in half an hour. I am assuming, of course, that you have a good fish stock in your freezer; if not, plan to make this after you've had a lobster or a supper of steamed mussels and have some of that intense lobster or mussel broth left. Otherwise use clam juice, diluted by half with water because it is quite strong.

WHAT YOU NEED

1 tablespoon olive oil

1 small onion, chopped

1 garlic clove, peeled and chopped

1 medium tomato, chopped

2 cups fish broth (see headnote)

A few fresh parsley stems

Pinch of fennel seeds

Salt and freshly ground pepper to taste

4 or 5 small clams

1 dozen mussels

A piece of leftover cooked or fresh fish, about 4 ounces*

A sprinkling of chopped parsley

2 slices French bread, toasted

A generous dollop of *Pistou* Sauce (see page 112)**

*Usually a fresh white fish is called for, but I have found that a piece of lightly cooked leftover salmon is fine, too.

**If you don't have any *pistou* on hand or time to make it, try mashing to a paste a small clove of garlic and a little salt, and then mixing that in with a tablespoon of mayonnaise. Whisk in a few pinches of paprika and a dash of hot pepper. Purists would not approve, but you can cheat a little when you're by yourself. Nobody is looking.

Heat the oil in a medium pot, and sauté the onion and garlic gently until softened. Add the tomato, sauté another minute, then pour in the fish stock and seasonings, tasting to judge how much salt and pepper you need. Simmer for about 20 minutes, and add the clams (if you are using fresh fish, slip that into the pot now); clams always take longer than mussels, so give the clams a few minutes before adding the mussels along with the piece of leftover fish. Sprinkle parsley over, and have alongside a couple of slices of toasted French bread with *pistou* on top.

Winter Bean Soup

Here's a soup to warm your heart even on the bleakest day of winter. Use it as a guideline, and make your own innovations according to what you have on hand. The beans are very nourishing, the meat accent lends heartiness, and the greens are healthy, giving balance and color. It's interesting how cooks of the past just knew these things instinctively.

1 tablespoon butter or vegetable oil	¼ cup cooked dried beans or lentils
1 small onion, or ¼ large onion	4 or 5 slices cooked sausage, or as many as you wish
1 new potato, sliced	Croutons, rubbed with garlic if you like, or a couple of slices French bread
2 cups broth, preferably meaty—beef, lamb, duck, or goose	
A handful of Swiss chard or spinach leaves	A sprinkling of Parmesan (optional)

Melt the butter in a small pot, and add the onion and potato. Sauté for a few minutes, and pour in the broth. Simmer for 30 minutes, covered. Add the greens during the last 5 minutes of cooking, as well as the dried beans. Stir in the sausage at the end, and heat through.

Serve in a big soup bowl with croutons and some (optional) Parmesan floating on top.

Variations

If you don't have any sausage, use some meat scraps—leftover lamb or pork or dark poultry meat.

Instead of cooked dried beans, which you may not have stashed away, try fresh fava beans. You have to shuck them and then peel off the skins of the beans, but you'll only need about a dozen for this soup, so it's not that hard—another advantage of cooking just for one.

COLD SUMMER SOUPS

In summer, I want a chilled soup that is quick to make and puts to good use some of the season's haul of tempting fruits and vegetables.

Cold Cucumber and Yogurt Soup

WHAT YOU NEED

A small Kirby pickling cucumber
1 scallion
⅔ cup chicken broth
¼ cup plain whole-milk yogurt
Salt and freshly ground pepper

A grating of fresh ginger
A generous sprinkling of chopped
    chives and fresh dill, if
    available

Peel the cucumber, and cut into chunks. Trim the scallion of coarse outer leaves, keeping the tender green; chop it and the white part into rough pieces. Put the cucumber and scallion along with the chicken broth and yogurt in a food processor or a blender, and spin until well blended. Season with salt and pepper and a grating of fresh ginger. Pour into a chilled soup bowl, and sprinkle the herbs on top.

Variation

Use fish stock instead of chicken broth, and add about ⅓ cup cooked salmon broken into flakes. Decrease the amount of yogurt to 2 teaspoons, and purée everything together in a blender or a food processor.

Cold Watermelon Soup

This is ideal to make when you've bought too much watermelon.

WHAT YOU NEED

A piece of watermelon, approximately 1 pound	½ lime
1 scallion	A sprinkling of chopped fresh mint
2 tablespoons Chablis	

Cut off the watermelon rind—you can save it for making pickles, if you're into that (I confess, I'm not). Using a melon ball, scoop out two balls of watermelon for garnish. Cut the rest of the melon into chunks. Trim the scallion, preserving the tender green, and chop roughly. Put the watermelon, scallion, and wine, along with several drops of lime juice, into a food processor or a blender, and purée. Taste and adjust flavors; you may want more lime juice. Turn into a chilled bowl and garnish with the watermelon balls and mint leaves.

Blueberry Soup

This is a soup I had years ago at an inn in Peacham, Vermont, when my husband, Evan, and I were looking for recipes for our book on new New England cooking. It is so delectable that every year now I celebrate the coming of the blueberries by making myself this soup. And, of course, I am blessed by having my cousin John tap our maple trees in the spring, so there is always maple syrup in my larder.

WHAT YOU NEED

¾ cup blueberries

1½ tablespoons maple syrup

2 tablespoons orange juice

Pinch of ground cinnamon

A few drops of lemon juice

¾ cup half-and-half, or equal
    parts milk and heavy cream

Put everything except the lemon juice and the half-and-half in a small saucepan. Heat, and when it comes to a boil remove from the heat and purée in a food processor or a blender. Add lemon juice to taste, and chill. Just before you're ready to eat, stir in the half-and-half, and then pour into a chilled bowl.

Three The Magic of Eggs—and the Seduction of Cheese

When you're cooking just for yourself, you'll find that eggs can be your best friend. They're always there waiting to be put to good use in an omelet or a frittata, or to be scrambled, baked, shirred, poached, or boiled (hard or soft). They marry well with all sorts of tasty bits that may be lurking in your refrigerator. So be creative with them, and flexible about using some of the ideas I offer here.

It's worth buying organic, cage-free eggs, or if you're in the country getting them directly from a good farm. And try not to keep them more than a week. You can ask for only half a carton.

Baked Eggs

Use a gratin dish that holds about 1 cup if you're baking only one egg, and a slightly larger dish if you want to do two.

WHAT YOU NEED

About 1 cup grated zucchini

Salt

2 teaspoons butter

About 3 small mushrooms, finely chopped

1 scallion, finely chopped

3 or 4 teaspoons heavy cream

1 or 2 large eggs

Freshly ground pepper

Gratings of Parmesan (optional)

Put the zucchini in a strainer, work ½ teaspoon salt into it, then set it over a bowl to drain.

Melt the butter in a small skillet, and sauté the chopped mushrooms and scallion for a minute. Squeeze the zucchini to eliminate as much juice as you can, then stir the grated strands into the pan. Pour in half the cream, and let cook gently for 3–4 minutes, until almost tender. Transfer the vegetables to a gratin dish, and with the back of a spoon make an indentation in the middle, then crack the egg into it. Season with a little more salt and some freshly ground pepper, and drizzle the rest of the cream on top. If you wish, sprinkle on some Parmesan. Bake in a pre-heated 350° oven for 15–18 minutes, until the egg is set.

Other Possibilities

Look in your fridge and you may find you have some leftover leafy vegetables, such as spinach or Swiss chard, or some broccoli or its more elegant cousin broccolini, or a winter root vegetable you could mash up—any of these would make a fine bed for our baked egg and could be put directly into the gratin dish and heated quickly in the microwave.

MICROWAVED EGGS

Speaking of the microwave—an instrument of cooking I seldom use—one day I had a yen for a baked egg over some leftover ratatouille. After heating up the vegetables in the microwave, I thought I'd try dropping the egg on top and microwaving for just 1 minute instead of baking. And it was miraculously good. That dish took less than 5 minutes to put on the table.

Shirred Egg with Chicken Liver

I've loved shirred eggs ever since I first sampled them in a Paris brasserie years ago. But I didn't know exactly how to make them until I came across the carefully instructive recipe in Julia Child's masterful tome, Mastering the Art of French Cooking, *where they were called* œufs sur le plat *or* œufs miroir *(in deference to their shimmering surface). Here's my favorite version, which I invariably make when I have plucked the packet of giblets from the cavity of a chicken. It should always include a plump liver—the cook's treat.*

WHAT YOU NEED

2 teaspoons butter (4, if using 2 eggs)

1 chicken liver, cut in half

1 small shallot or 1 scallion, chopped (or both, which I prefer)

A splash of dry sherry

1 or 2 large eggs

Salt and freshly ground pepper

Preheat the broiler. Melt the butter in a small heatproof gratin pan. When it is sizzling, toss in the chicken liver, sear for only a minute, then add the shallot and/or scallion and cook quickly, tossing, for another ½ minute. Splash in the sherry, let cook for a few seconds, until syrupy, then carefully break the egg right into the pan. Salt and pepper everything, and let cook over medium heat until the egg has just begun to set. Spoon the little bit of pan juice over the egg, and slip onto a rack about 6 inches under the broiler to finish cooking, just until the egg is set. Baste again, and eat from the gratin pan with some toasted bread to mop up the browned bits and juice.

Other Possibilities

Ham and sausage are also wonderful with shirred eggs, and you could do a vegetarian version with some onion and sweet pepper or some leftover ratatouille, if you have any.

Omelets

Don't let yourself be frightened at the prospect of making an omelet. The more you make, the easier it will be, and it only takes minutes to produce a seductive oval mound of yellow eggs wrapped around a filling that provides just the right complement. An omelet can make a whole meal and is a great receptacle for whatever little bits of things you've stored in your fridge. So I'll give only proportions and suggestions for various fillings, not specific directions for preparing each one. That way, you can use mine as guidelines to make your own.

It is important to have a good nonstick omelet pan. Mine is 6½ inches in diameter at the base and 8 inches across the top, the size I like for a two-egg omelet, and I reserve it for only that purpose. If you prefer a slightly thinner, more spread-out omelet, get a pan with an 8-inch bottom diameter.

WHAT YOU NEED

About 3 tablespoons filling (see suggestions in box opposite)
2 teaspoons butter

2 large eggs
Salt and freshly ground pepper

If the filling you plan to use is cooked, either heat it up in the omelet pan with a little butter or olive oil and then turn it out onto a small dish and keep it in a warm spot, or heat it briefly in the microwave. If you're dealing with raw ingredients that need cooking, use a separate pan, and have everything cooked and ready to go as you start your omelet.

When you're ready, heat the butter in the omelet pan over medium-high heat. Meanwhile, quickly crack the eggs into a small bowl, season with a good pinch of salt and several grindings of pepper, and beat with a fork until the yolks and whites are just blended. The butter in the pan should be hot and sizzling, and as the large bubbles start to subside, you'll know you're ready to go. Pour the eggs in, and let them set for just 10 seconds. With the flat of your fork against the bottom of the pan, vigorously move the mass of eggs all around. Let them set again for just another few seconds, and then with the tines of the fork pull the parts of the egg that have set around the rim toward the center, and tilt the pan slightly so that the uncooked, liquidy parts flow onto the bare spots and set. This whole process should take only about 1 minute. Now spoon the filling across the center of the eggs, and give the pan a very firm jerk or two, so that the egg mass at the far edge of the pan flips forward onto the filling (you can nudge it with a spatula if it needs help). Turn the omelet out onto a warm plate, letting the filled part settle on the plate first, and then tilt the pan further and flip the remaining, uncovered part over the top. And, voilà, you have a perfect omelet. And if it isn't quite perfection, *tant pis.* Only you will know—and it will taste delicious.

Ideas for Omelet Fillings

- A few leftover cooked asparagus spears cut in quarters and warmed in butter
- Leftover cooked spinach or other greens, such as Swiss chard, turnip, or beet greens, warmed in a little olive oil
- Eggplant, particularly leftover ratatouille (page 132)
- Roasted peppers
- Mushrooms, sautéed, or use a couple of tablespoons of duxelles (page 138)
- One or two roasted or boiled small potatoes, particularly good with cooked leeks or artichoke hearts or sorrel
- Cheeses: A tablespoon of fresh cheese is always a nice complement to any of the above vegetables. Grated aged cheeses like Cheddar, Gouda, Cantal, Parmigiano-Reggiano, or a Grana Padano (just look in your cheese bin and see what's there) are all yummy as an accent with other fillings. Mix and match as you please, or make just a pure cheese omelet, sprinkling some on top as well as using a generous amount as filling.
- Meaty and fishy accents: Try a little shredded ham or prosciutto, cooked crumbled sausage, roughly chopped chicken livers, creamed chicken, or turkey. For fishy accents, if you have some leftover salmon, flake it and mix with some herbs or a little green sauce; shrimp and scallops, perked up the same way, are also good. Bland fish is disappointing, but smoked fish—salmon, trout, finnan haddie—all make a fine foil for eggs.

Frittatas

The difference between a frittata and an omelet, as I see it, is that the frittata cooks very slowly and will be somewhat more firm, so that it can suspend a number of different garnishes nicely arrayed in a pattern, with their flavors complementing one another. I always slip my frittata under the broiler at the end, so that the cheese scattered on top browns. This is another dish that welcomes improvisation.

WHAT YOU NEED

1 large leek, white part only, cut in quarters lengthwise

1 tablespoon butter or light olive oil or a combination, or more if needed

¼ large red or green bell pepper, cut into strips

2 large eggs

Salt and freshly ground pepper

1 thin slice prosciutto or country or Serrano ham, cut into strips

1 cooked new potato, sliced

Freshly grated Parmesan

Put the leek pieces in your nonstick omelet or cast-iron pan, and barely cover with water. Bring to a boil, and cook until the water has evaporated, about 5 minutes. Push aside, trying to keep the leek quarters intact, add the butter or oil to the pan, and lay in the pepper strips. Cook another few minutes, then remove to a plate with a spatula.

Crack the eggs into a bowl, season with salt and pepper, and mix well with a fork. Set the pan over low heat, adding just a little more fat if needed, and pour the eggs in. Now arrange the leeks and peppers and ham strips in spokes, and tuck slices of potato in between. Add a little more salt and pepper, and cook, covered, very slowly for 8–10 minutes, until set but still a little runny on top. Grate a light coating of Parmesan over it, and slip under a preheated broiler just long enough to solidify the eggs and brown lightly.

Other Ideas

I like to use vegetables that can be arranged in a spoke pattern. Asparagus and a slim zucchini quartered lengthwise are good, as well as different colors of bell pepper, but you don't have to let the aesthetics dictate. Small cooked artichoke hearts are wonderful with potatoes here—of course with some scallion or onion—but they will take longer in the initial cooking, 15–20 minutes. You can cook your potato along with the artichokes, if you prefer. And mushrooms are a delight, particularly if you have some attractive wild varieties, like golden chanterelles. The potato I feel is almost a must; it gives substance to the dish and, along with the Serrano ham, if you happen to have that, a distinctly Spanish accent—a delicious, attractive meal all in one.

Steamed Egg(s) Nestled in a Bed of Greens

What could be simpler than tossing tender greens into a wok and nestling an egg or two on top so they steam together? And it looks so ravishing on the plate.

WHAT YOU NEED

2 handfuls of tender greens
    (spinach, beet greens, Swiss
    chard, turnip greens, cress, or
    a combination)
Salt

1 tablespoon light olive oil
1 garlic clove, peeled and slivered
1 or 2 large eggs
Freshly ground pepper

If your greens are more mature, trim off the stalks and cut these into 1-inch pieces. Drop the stems into a pot full of boiling, lightly salted

water, and cook them for 4 or 5 minutes. Drain and run cold water over them. Tear the leaves into smaller pieces.

If the greens are young, the above step is not necessary. Heat a wok or a large sauté pan (use a pan that has a tight-fitting cover), pour in the oil, and when it is hot drop in the slivers of garlic. Cook, stirring, over quite high heat, and before the garlic starts to brown, toss in all the greens (plus the blanched stems of the older ones). Stir-fry for 1 minute, than add about ½ cup water, and cook until almost tender. Taste to gauge when done. Make an indentation in the center of the greens (or two indentations if using two eggs), and crack the egg(s) into it.

Check to be sure there's enough water left to steam; if not, add a little more. Sprinkle on salt and pepper, cover, and steam over medium heat. In 3 minutes, the egg(s) should be just nicely done and almost all the liquid boiled away. Remove carefully to a plate, using a large slotted spatula so the remaining liquid runs off. Center the egg(s) in the middle of the plate, with the greens around.

Variations

The egg(s) could nestle on a bed of cut-up asparagus or some grated zucchini, or a combination of vegetables cut into matchsticks.

Hard-Boiled Eggs

A few hard-boiled eggs are a good staple to have on hand to mix into a salad, garnish a plate of cold vegetables, make a quick sandwich for lunch, or use in my favorite Sauce Gribiche (see page 160). So when you're boiling an egg, do one or two extra.

I have found over the years that the best way to prepare perfect, easy-to-peel hard-boiled eggs is to prick them first, piercing through the shell at the more rounded end, put them in a pot with enough cold water to cover generously, and bring them to a vigorous boil. Immediately turn off the heat and cover the pot. Leave for 20 minutes or a little less, and then plunge them into cold water. Peel them right away, cracking the shells all over and removing the peel under cold running water. Those I'm not using immediately I wrap separately and snugly in plastic wrap and refrigerate; they will keep for almost a week.

Variations

DEVILED EGGS

These are best prepared soon after peeling. Just cut the egg in half lengthwise, and scoop out the yolk. Mash it with a fork, and work in ⅛ teaspoon Dijon mustard, 1 teaspoon or more mayonnaise (if you are lucky enough to have some homemade mayo on hand, by all means use it—see recipe on page 111), a generous pinch of salt, and a couple of turns of the pepper grinder. Fill the cavity of the egg-white halves with the mashed yolk, and sprinkle a little paprika on top, or some finely chopped fresh herbs, such as chives, parsley, tarragon, basil—you make the call. Other seasonings might include a pinch of anchovy paste, a chopped scallion, a little pesto, some finely chopped pimientos, or an olive, whatever strikes your fancy.

EGG SALAD

For one, you will probably want two hard-boiled eggs, peeled and chopped, mixed with 1½–2 tablespoons mayonnaise (for a sandwich, one large egg will suffice). Use any of the seasonings suggested above. I find that I like the crunch of a little chopped celery (fennel is also good), or some red or green bell pepper. Again, experiment.

Eggs Benedict

Once you've made your small amount of hollandaise sauce, it is simple to put together that heavenly creation, egg (or eggs) Benedict, and enjoy it all alone for a Sunday brunch.

WHAT YOU NEED

1 recipe Hollandaise for One
    (recipe follows)
Salt
1 English muffin (or, if you
    haven't one, use a slice of
    good white bread)

A little butter
1 or 2 slices ham or prosciutto,
    at room temperature
1 or 2 fresh large eggs
A few grindings of pepper
A sprinkling of paprika

If the hollandaise has cooled, warm it slowly in a small flameproof bowl set over a pan of barely simmering water, whisking. When it is warm, set aside off heat, whisking occasionally, while you prepare the egg(s). Bring a small pot (or a larger one if using two eggs) of salted water to a boil, then lower the heat to a simmer. Meanwhile, split the English muffin, then toast and butter it. Warm the ham or prosciutto in a pan, or quickly in a microwave, and lay on top of the muffin on a plate. Crack 1 egg carefully into a small cup, and slip it into the barely simmering water. (If you are doing 2 eggs, slip the second one in in the same way.) Keep the heat at a gentle simmer, and poach the egg(s) for 4 minutes, spooning the simmering water over the tops now and then. Scoop up the egg(s) with a slotted spoon, let the water drip off, and center on an English-muffin half. Salt lightly, and grind some pepper on top, then spoon on as much hollandaise as you want. Sprinkle on a light dusting of paprika.

Variation

Instead of ham or prosciutto, use a slice of smoked salmon, with a few capers sprinkled over it.

Hollandaise for One

Every now and then, I get a yearning for a bit of warm, smooth, buttery-lemony hollandaise sauce to dip artichoke leaves into, to top a poached egg with so that I can enjoy that delicious flavor play of eggs Benedict, or to spread over a piece of grilled salmon—or other fish. But to make a small amount for just one or two servings of this tricky sauce (and then reheat what's leftover)? Impossible, the pros would say. However, where there's a will, there's a way. So I experimented and managed to work out a method that served my purposes beautifully. Here it is.

WHAT YOU NEED

1 large egg yolk, at room temperature

4 tablespoons very cold butter, cut in 12 pieces

About 1½ teaspoons fresh lemon juice

Salt

Makes a generous ⅓ cup

Warm the yolk slowly in a small, heavy pot, such as Le Creuset, set in a sauté pan of barely simmering water, whisking vigorously. When the yolk turns lemon-colored and starts to thicken, add the very cold butter pieces one by one, continuing to whisk steadily. As soon as one piece of butter is incorporated, whisk in the next one. If at any point the sauce starts to bubble or separate, immediately remove the pot from the warmth of the sauté pan and set it into a pan of icy water. But you should not have this difficulty if you work slowly and patiently. When all the butter has been absorbed and the sauce is warm and thick, season with at least a teaspoon of lemon juice and salt to your taste.

To store any remaining hollandaise, put it in a very small saucerlike bowl and film with plastic wrap. It will keep refrigerated for several days. To warm up, let it come to room temperature slowly, then put the sauce in a small pot over warm water, and whisk furiously. It should recover its creamy consistency. If it starts to curdle, quickly remove the pan from the heat and whisk a teaspoon of cold cream into the sauce. Taste and add a little more lemon juice if needed.

Mayonnaise

Treat yourself once in a while to homemade mayonnaise prepared in a food processor. This simple version is delicious and light—and it takes about 5 minutes to whip up. It will keep about a week, but mine usually vanishes before that, particularly if I use some of it to make the Mediterranean Pistou *Sauce that follows.*

WHAT YOU NEED

1 large egg

½ teaspoon Dijon mustard

½ lemon

Salt

About ¾ cup light extra-virgin olive oil

Spin the egg, mustard, a few drops of lemon juice, and a small pinch of salt in the food processor long enough to blend well. With the machine going, pour the olive oil in, a few drops at a time to begin, then in a steady stream. When the mayonnaise has thickened and you have used up almost all the oil, taste and adjust: you will need several drops more lemon juice, and a little more salt, and perhaps, if the sauce doesn't seem thick enough, a little more olive oil blended in. That's it.

Variations

If you don't have a food processor and want to make the mayonnaise by hand, use just the egg yolk instead of the whole egg. Drop the yolk in a small shallow bowl and beat constantly with a fork in one hand as you slowly add the olive oil, in droplets at first, then in a steady stream, until thickened.

To make a simple version of a *Pistou* Sauce that's particularly good with bouillabaisse (page 91), or swirled into a vegetable soup, or added to a green sauce, smash, remove the peel from, and chop fine 2 fat garlic cloves. Sprinkle a large pinch of salt on top, and mash with the flat of your large knife until you have a paste. Stir that into about ½ cup of your mayonnaise. Mix in about a quarter of a large red bell pepper, roasted, peel removed, and cut into small dice (or use a roasted pepper from a jar), and season with a large pinch of sweet paprika and a small pinch (at least that's all I like) of hot pepper flakes. Taste, and adjust the seasonings to your liking.

Half an Egg?

An old wives' tale is that you can't halve an egg. So many single cooks will pass up a recipe simply because reducing it would entail using half an egg. But all you need do to make this feat possible is to crack a large egg into a small jar and shake it up. When the white and yolk are well blended, you'll have 3 tablespoons. So, for your half-egg, simply extract 1½ tablespoons and use it as called for. Just refrigerate the remaining egg in the tightly lidded jar, and use it for a glaze or add to scrambled eggs or an omelet next time you make one. Or find another recipe that, when reduced to serve one, calls for half an egg.

Strata: A Savory Custard

This vegetable custard calls for the same ingredients as the individual timbales that I learned to make as a youngster from my aunt Marian in Vermont and have relished ever since. It's a good way to use up yesterday's baguette and a leftover vegetable, to say nothing of that fallback ingredient, a piece of ham. Here I put everything into a 1½ cup ceramic baking dish that has a 4½-inch diameter and it fills the dish, coming out of the oven puffy and lightly tanned. It's easier than having to unmold the individual timbales, and, of course, I eat it right from the dish as soon as it has cooled long enough not to burn my tongue.

WHAT YOU NEED

About ½ cup stale bread, torn in small pieces, any tough crusts removed

¼ cup milk

A slice of ham, enough to fill the bottom of the dish (leftover baked ham is particularly good here; see page 60)

A little soft butter

3 spears cooked asparagus

Salt

1 large egg

¼ cup mixture of milk and cream or half-and-half

Freshly ground pepper

A couple of fresh sage leaves or fresh basil torn (optional)

About 1 generous tablespoon grated cheese, Parmesan or aged Cheddar or Swiss

Put the bread in a bowl with the milk to soak for about 5 minutes, and then squeeze it through your fingers to dissolve the crumbs in the milk. Meanwhile, place the ham on the bottom of a single-portion buttered baking dish and lay the asparagus spears, cut in half, over the ham. Salt lightly. Beat the egg with the milk-cream mixture, add a little salt and freshly ground pepper, and pour that over the asparagus. Arrange optional sage leaves on top and sprinkle on the grated cheese. Bake in a preheated 350° oven for 25 minutes. Let settle for a few minutes out of the oven before you dive in.

Variations

You can use any number of cooked vegetables as a base here, whatever you may have lurking in the refrigerator—some broccoli (or broccolini) florets, grated zucchini, artichoke hearts, or braised fennel. If you use a leafy vegetable like spinach or chard, squeeze out all the water first.

Cheese Soufflé

The other day, at a French brasserie across the street from our offices in New York, I ordered their single soufflé served with a green salad. It was a perfect lunch, and I went away wondering why I didn't make soufflés anymore. It's not only a good way to use up some of the bits of cheeses you may have around, as well as other leftovers that need reincarnation, but it's lovely to behold and scrumptious to eat. But to make it for one? I was sure it could be done, so I purchased myself a one-person, fluted soufflé dish, 2¾ inches high and 4 inches in diameter, and proved that it could. My recipe for one is based on the eight pages of careful instructions that Julia Child devoted to making the perfect soufflé in Mastering the Art of French Cooking.

WHAT YOU NEED

½ teaspoon soft butter and
    1 tablespoon grated Parmesan
    for preparing the mold
2 teaspoons butter
1 tablespoon all-purpose flour
⅓ cup milk
Large pinch of salt

Small pinch of paprika
1 egg yolk
2 egg whites
⅓ tightly packed cup grated
    cheese (an aged Cheddar,
    a Swiss cheese, an aged
    mountain cheese)

Smear the soft butter around the inside of your mold, and sprinkle the Parmesan around the sides and bottom. Preheat the oven to 425°. Melt the 2 teaspoons butter in a small pot, and stir in the flour. Let cook over low heat for a minute, then remove from the heat for a moment's rest. Now pour in the milk, whisking vigorously, and return to low heat to simmer for 1 minute, stirring constantly as the sauce thickens. Season with the salt and paprika. Again remove from the heat, and whisk in the egg yolk. Put the egg whites in a clean bowl, and beat until they form soft peaks. Add a dollop of the egg whites to the sauce, and mix in along with about half the cheese. Now fold in the rest of the egg whites and the cheese, and transfer everything to the prepared mold. Set in the middle of the oven, and turn the heat down to 375°. Bake for 18 minutes, until the top is lightly browned and the soufflé has risen.

Variations

You can make this single soufflé using about 3 tablespoons of a finely chopped cooked green vegetable or a couple of tablespoons of mushroom duxelles (page 138), or some minced ham, in which case you would want to use only a tablespoon of a milder cheese, such as Swiss.

Grating cheese with a carpenter's rasp

All About Cheese

I'm afraid that a lot of single cooks are wary of buying cheese, because they usually have to purchase a whole round or square or a big wedge and they're stuck with more than they can eat up. But remember that cheese is fermented milk, so it really doesn't matter if it ferments further in your refrigerator and develops some mold. You can just scrape it off, and you'll often find that the cheese is perfectly edible. Soft-ripened cheeses do tend to develop a sour taste if kept *too* long, so eat those first.

If you can, try to get your cheeses from a specialty cheese shop, and develop a friendship with whoever is in charge. He or she will usually give a sample of a cheese you may want to buy, and will tell you whether it should be eaten right away or stored longer before opening. Often, too, he will cut one of those rounds and let you have just half, and will certainly slice a large aged cheese to your specifications. Tasting is the only way you'll learn about a new cheese.

For many, many years, Evan and I bought all our cheese at Eddy Edelman's Ideal Cheese, a little shop on mid-Manhattan's East Side. It was a ritual: we would meet there on my way home, Evan bringing our dog along for a treat, and we would talk and sample Eddy's latest offerings. He made a point of not overstocking and would never dream of selling an over-the-hill cheese. And he liked to get our reactions to new imports. He would alert us when the true seasonal Vacherin arrived—made in winter, when the cows in the Alps are fed on the last crop of hay—so rich, creamy, and oozing that it has to be eaten with a spoon.

There aren't many small, personal cheese shops left, but it's still worth trying to connect with someone knowledgeable. The choices we have today are wonderfully inviting, but at the same time overwhelming.

Since I end my dinner with cheese almost every night that I'm alone, I want variety on my plate, so I try to have at least two or three types stored away. I love all the soft-ripened cheeses—the more assertive in taste and aroma the better—such as Époisses, Livarot, Rebluchon, Alsatian Münster, and hard-to-find Soumaintrain, as well as the gentler Taleggio, and the farm-made Bries and Camemberts. But paired with one of those I like the blues—true Roquefort, Bleu de Bresse, Gorgonzola, especially the *dolce,* a Stilton at Christmastime, and, more recently, the happy discovery of a Bayley Hazen Blue (coincidentally, named after my Bailey ancestor), made in the Northeast Kingdom of Vermont at Jasper Hill Farm. And I wouldn't be without some of the semi-aged cheeses—a lovely Cantal from the French Alps, some real Emmental, an aged Gouda, or Cheddar, which can be transformed by spending some time in a cave before shipping.

My cheese collection always includes a generous hunk of Parmesan, Parmigiano-Reggiano. When I first replenish my supply, I break off a good piece to eat with an apple, a pear, or figs—we forget how good aged cheese can be with fruit. But mostly I use the Parmesan for grating on just about everything. I find that the carpenter's rasp is a godsend for grating hard cheese. It makes it so effortless, and the resulting mound of cheese is so fluffy you have to remember to press it down if you are measuring (but who wants to measure cheese?). And remember when you get to the end of your Parmesan to save the rind. It transforms a pot of simmering soup.

I haven't touched on the explosion of fresh cheeses available, but they are often a good investment for the lone cook; they tend to come in small sizes, and are an asset in so many things—lunch salads, sandwiches, pastas, baked dishes. There's a whole world to explore in cheese, particularly with small artisan cheesemakers springing up all around this country, making a surprising variety of cheeses from cow's, goat's, sheep's, and buffalo milk, many of which are first-rate. Get information on the Internet, and go to farmers' markets to seek them out.

HOW TO STORE CHEESE

Purists will say that you should only store cheese in paper wrapping, but if you keep several kinds a considerable amount of time, the paper gets dank and tacky. So I usually start out with the paper the cheese comes in, and then switch to plastic wrap. I also keep my cheeses in a large plastic box in the refrigerator, so I can find them easily and so their odor doesn't permeate other foods. Once in a while I have even frozen a cheese, if I'm saddled with a big hunk. The more delicate semi-softs don't fare as well this way, but the semi-hard and aged cheeses don't suffer too much from freezing. And it's better than throwing them out.

HOW TO SERVE CHEESE

- Always remove cheeses from the fridge about 1 hour before eating so that their flavors can blossom at room temperature.
- I prefer to serve cheese, as the French do, after the main course, either alone or with salad or fruit.
- Cheese is a great flavor enhancer and there are many recipes throughout this book that call for cheese. So if you have overstocked and need ideas on how to use up your excess cheese, look for suggestions in soups, salads, omelets, and quiches as well as dishes such as soufflés and stratas. And if you feel like putting cheese center stage, treat yourself to a supper of molten cheese on toast.

WELSH RABBIT

WHAT YOU NEED

1 tablespoon butter

1 egg yolk

3 tablespoons beer or ale or white wine

A pinch of dry mustard

5 or 6 drops of Worcestershire sauce, if available

A pinch of salt

2 ounces cheese (Cheddar, aged Gouda, Caerphilly, French mountain cheese are all good but use what you have) cut in small, thin pieces or grated on the coarse holes of a grater

1 slice bread, toasted

Warm the butter in a small heavy pot set over a pan of barely simmering water. When it has melted, whisk in the egg yolk, beer, and seasonings. Continue to whisk until lightly thickened, then add the cheese in small increments, whisking as each addition is melted and incorporated. When all the cheese has been used and the sauce has the thickness of a hollandaise, remove from the heat and spoon the molten cheese over the toast.

Four Improvising with Vegetables, Salads, and Sauces

An Artichoke *Toute Seule*
Stuffed Eggplant
Stuffed Portobello
Stuffed Baked Potato
THE GIFT OF CHANTERELLES
Zucchini Pancakes
Corn and Salmon Pancakes
Moussaka
Ratatouille
Purée of Parsnips (or Celery Root) and Potatoes
A Potato Dish for Julia
DUXELLES: A WAY OF PRESERVING YOUR MUSHROOMS
Braised Endive with Ham and Cheese
Roasted Asparagus with a Sesame Vinaigrette
   Second round: BLA (Bacon, Lettuce, and Asparagus Sandwich)
Roasted Celery Root (Celeriac)
Celery Rémoulade
OTHER GOOD ROASTED VEGETABLES
Stir-Fried Vegetables
Chicken Salad
Asian-Accented Chicken Salad
PRESERVING AN AVOCADO
Vinaigrette
Blue Cheese Dressing

SALAD GREENS—KEEPING THEM FRESH

Roasted Beet, Arugula, and Endive Salad with Blue Cheese
   Dressing

Fennel, Apple, and Walnut Salad

Tabbouleh

Warm Potato Salad with Sausage

Fish Salad

Pesto

Winter Green Sauce

Sauce Gribiche

Ed Giobbi's Fresh Mint Sauce

Tomato Sauce

Cucumber Raita

Cream Sauce

So often when you're cooking for yourself, you want something light. You may have had a heavy lunch, or eaten too much the night before, and feel like nothing more than a simple vegetable or a salad, or some cold meat or chicken—perked up, of course, with a little piquant sauce to save it from second-day doldrums.

Or you may have some leftover vegetables that served as accompaniments and are all cooked and ready to find new life in dishes such as a tian or a strata (a savory custard), a pancake, a salad, even a sandwich. Vegetables are great carriers, too. They take well to being stuffed with delicious tidbits and baked. So here is a vegetable, salad, and sauce world to explore, and I hope it will stimulate your own improvisations.

An Artichoke *Toute Seule*

There is something pleasantly sensual and mindful about eating an artichoke all alone, dunking each leaf in a tart, buttery sauce and scraping off that little bit of flesh, then getting to the bottom and carefully removing the prickly this- tles to the heart. I remember loving this as an adolescent and always asking for an artichoke when I knew I would be home alone and could relish each bite. If you're feeling in a cooking mood, make yourself a little hollandaise sauce (page 110) to go with this treat.

WHAT YOU NEED

　1 large artichoke (look for one with tight leaves)

　DIPPING SAUCE (IF NOT USING HOLLANDAISE)
　2 tablespoons butter, melted
　½ lemon

You can either steam or boil a big artichoke. I prefer steaming, because the artichoke gets less waterlogged, and it doesn't take much longer. So get a big pot of water going, with a steamer set up inside it, while prepar- ing the artichoke. Trim off the small outer leaves and cut off the stem close to the base. I always keep the stems for a salad, so I shave off the stringy outside and steam the stem alongside the artichoke, retrieving it when it is tender (20–25 minutes). After about 40 minutes of steaming, the arti- choke should be done; test by pulling off a leaf: if it pulls off easily, the base is tender. Drain well. Squeeze as much fresh lemon juice as you like into the melted butter, mix well, and put sauce in a little dipping bowl.

While you're at it, why not cook a second artichoke and have it later in the week with a vinaigrette (page 149)? I often take an artichoke to the office for lunch.

Stuffed Eggplant

Eggplant is a particularly good receptacle for leftovers, such as cooked rice or grains and the remains of a roast. When I'm using eggplant, I usually roast it in the morning, or the night before I'm going to stuff it. Then it takes only about 40 minutes to be ready to enjoy. This stuffed eggplant is good hot, warm, or at room temperature, so you can to take it on a picnic, or to the park for lunch.

WHAT YOU NEED

1 small eggplant, about 5 inches long

½ cup cooked rice

½ cup cooked meat (lamb, preferably, or pork, beef, leftover meatloaf), chopped fine

2 scallions, diced fine

2 teaspoons toasted pine nuts

2 canned tomatoes (preferably San Marzano), squeezed, or, if in season, 2 small fresh tomatoes, diced

Pinch of cinnamon

Salt and freshly ground pepper

2 tablespoons fresh breadcrumbs

Extra-virgin olive oil

Prick the eggplant all over with a fork, and put it in a preheated 425° oven for 35 minutes. Remove, and let cool. Slice the eggplant in half lengthwise, and scoop out the flesh, leaving a comfortable border of skin and flesh all around. Chop the eggplant flesh you have extracted, and mix it in a bowl with the rice, meat, scallions, pine nuts, and tomatoes. Season with cinnamon, salt, and pepper. Spoon this filling back into the eggplant shells, mounding it up in the middle, and arrange the halves in a shallow baking pan that just holds them. Sprinkle the breadcrumbs on top, and drizzle onto them a little olive oil. Bake in a preheated 400° oven for 30–35 minutes, until tender and browned on top.

Variation

Stuff green peppers or zucchini in the same way, using the same general proportions. I like to blanch both these vegetables for a couple of minutes in boiling water before I fill them and bake them.

Stuffed Portobello

The large portobello mushroom makes a natural saucerlike container for tasty fillings. For modest appetites, one amply stuffed big mushroom will make a satisfying lunch or supper dish, but if you're really hungry, make two.

WHAT YOU NEED

1 large portobello mushroom, about 4½ inches in diameter
2 tablespoons butter
1 garlic clove, peeled and slivered
Salt and freshly ground pepper
Herbs: 1 heaping tablespoon chopped fresh parsley, chives, tarragon leaves, or sage if available

Meat accent: 1 tablespoon or more of crumbled cooked sausage, chopped ham, crumbled cooked bacon, or shredded prosciutto
Olive oil
½ cup fresh breadcrumbs

Cut the stem from the mushroom, and trim off any tough part. Wipe off dirt with a damp towel, and chop the stem into small dice. Melt the butter in a small skillet, and sauté the garlic and diced mushroom stem gently for about 5 minutes, to soften. Season with salt and pepper and fold in the herbs and meat. Rub a little olive oil all over the mushroom cap, and season with salt and pepper. Spoon the stuffing into the saucerlike gill side of the mushroom, tucking it in all around and mounding it in the center. Sprinkle the breadcrumbs on top. Place on a shallow baking dish in a preheated 350° oven for 30 minutes, at which point the top should be browned and crispy.

Stuffed Baked Potato

There is something about a baked potato that is so comforting that many of us eating alone enjoy making a meal of it. You can enhance it with whatever seems appealing—a generous dollop or two of sour cream or yogurt or butter, some chopped scallions, a few tasty mushrooms (or use mushroom duxelles, page 138), and/or a bit of leftover green vegetable. Some like a melty cheese or a strong accent, such as anchovy and olives, and if you happen to have some leftover ratatouille or fried eggplant and peppers, they marry well with the mealy roasted Idaho. Also, bacon, ham, or a bit of cracklings will add a meat accent, if you want that.

Since a large potato takes about an hour to bake in the oven, a good way of hurrying it along is to microwave it on high for 7 minutes, then put it into a 400° oven to crisp for about 10 minutes. When it is tender—pierce with the point of a knife to make sure—slit the top open, squeeze the hot potato to open it up, and spoon as much stuffing as you like into it. The filling should be at room temperature.

The Gift of Chanterelles

The summer of 2008 was a temperamental one, typical of the Northeast Kingdom of Vermont, with bursts of sunshine snatched away by sudden showers. But it was good weather for the wild mushrooms, and my friends Nova and Les, who are so skilled at unearthing their secret beds, brought me a huge boxful containing at least 5 pounds of golden chanterelles. Here's what I made with them, trying to capture their flavor in different ways and not wanting to waste a precious morsel.

Always clean wild mushrooms just before using them. Don't dump them in a bowl of water. Simply use a soft brush and a damp paper towel to remove any dirt, and trim off the hard, woody stem ends (and save them for soup). You'll find recipes for these dishes throughout the book that you can adapt.

- Sautéed mushrooms enfolded in crêpes
- A mushroom, shallot, and red-wine pan sauce for a loin strip steak
- A small mushroom quiche
- A poached egg nestled in sautéed young spinach leaves and chanterelles
- A tagine of beef, eggplant, and chanterelles
- A strata—a savory custard with vegetables and cheese
- An omelet filled with sautéed chanterelles
- A mushroom risotto
- Roasted large chanterelle caps, rubbed with olive oil and a little salt and placed in a hot oven for 10 minutes (they could be stuffed, too)

Zucchini Pancakes

Anyone who has a garden knows about the pressure to eat up the zucchini you've planted. You hate to see it go to waste. But the advantage to growing your own is that you can harvest the zucchini while they are still very young and have a more intense flavor (and you can use the male blossoms, too). So here's one more delicious way of appreciating this prolific vegetable. You can leave out the prosciutto and peppers if you like, but they do add considerable zest.

WHAT YOU NEED

1 or 2 small zucchini, grated to make about 1 cup

Salt

1 egg

3 tablespoons all-purpose flour

1 scallion, finely chopped

A few chopped fresh parsley and/or basil leaves

1 slice prosciutto, torn into small pieces (optional)

2 slim strips red or orange bell pepper, cut into small dice (optional)

Light olive oil

Garnish (optional): 3 or 4 squash blossoms

Spread out the grated zucchini on a towel, and sprinkle salt generously over it. After 5 minutes or so, pat dry to extract some of the juice. Beat the egg lightly in a bowl, and add the grated zucchini, the flour, scallion, and herbs, and the optional prosciutto and pepper pieces. Heat enough oil in a medium skillet to film it generously, and when it's hot, gather half the zucchini batter in your hand and plop it into the pan, flattening it slightly with a spatula. Do the same to make a second pancake, and cook them over medium heat. When the pancakes are brown on the bottom, turn and brown the other side. Remove them to a warm plate. If you have a few squash blossoms, fry them in a little butter in the same pan, flattening them with a spatula—they'll be done in a few seconds. Toss them on top of the pancakes.

Corn and Salmon Pancakes

I concocted these pancakes one night when I happened to have an ear of corn left over and a small piece of salmon I'd cooked the night before. It turned out to be a lovely, natural marriage of flavors.

WHAT YOU NEED

A small piece of cooked salmon, about 2 ounces

1 egg, beaten

Kernels scraped from 1 ear of cooked corn

1 teaspoon Wondra quick-mixing flour, plus a little more for dusting

1 or 2 scallions, finely chopped

Salt and freshly ground pepper

1 tablespoon butter

Chopped fresh parsley and/or basil, tarragon, or some other fresh, compatible herb

Flake the salmon, and break it into small pieces. Mix it with the egg, corn, instant flour, and scallions, and season with salt, several grindings of pepper, and a sprinkling of the chopped herbs. If you have time, let the mixture rest in the refrigerator for about 30 minutes; it will be a little easier to handle, but it's not necessary (and if your pancake doesn't hold together perfectly, only you will notice it). Melt the butter in a skillet, and with your hands shape half of the batter into a cake. When the butter is sizzling, gently slip the pancake into the pan. Make a second cake with the remaining batter, and cook the two cakes over medium heat until they are lightly browned on the bottom, then turn them and cook the other side. The pancakes are good with a green salad garnished with cucumbers and sweet cherry tomatoes. Scatter the remaining herbs over the pancakes.

Moussaka

Here's another way of giving leftover lamb new life. I'd always thought that this sumptuous Middle Eastern dish that envelops lamb in eggplant was quite a production, but done this way it takes less than half an hour to put together and is worth every minute of effort.

WHAT YOU NEED

1 small eggplant*
1 tablespoon olive oil
Salt
1 tablespoon vegetable oil
1 small or ½ medium onion, chopped
2 medium tomatoes, chopped
Pinch of hot pepper
Pinch of sugar (optional)

¾ cup cooked lamb, preferably rare, either chopped by hand into very small pieces or roughly ground in a food processor
Sprig of fresh parsley, chopped
About 3 tablespoons breadcrumbs
Dusting of grated Parmesan

*If you can't find a small eggplant, use a medium one and, after broiling, put away at least half the slices for tomorrow's lunch. I find eggplant delicious in a pita along with slices of fresh tomato.

Trim the ends off the eggplant, and slice crosswise into ¼- to ⅓-inch slices. Brush lightly with olive oil, and sprinkle a little salt on both sides. Line your broiling pan with Silpat or aluminum foil, and spread the slices on it. Slide under a preheated broiler, and cook for about 5 minutes on each side, until lightly browned. Stack, and cover with aluminum foil.

Meanwhile, heat the vegetable oil in a small pan, and sauté the onion for about 5 minutes, then add the tomatoes, hot pepper, and sugar (optional), and a sprinkling of salt. Sauté another 5 minutes, then add the lamb and parsley, and cook everything together until the juice from the tomatoes is somewhat reduced. Spread three or four slices of eggplant on the bottom of a single-serving shallow baking dish, top with most of the lamb and tomatoes, then spread another layer of eggplant over, and the remaining juices and bits from the lamb mix. Sprinkle the breadcrumbs and cheese on top, and bake for 10 minutes in a preheated 375° oven. Slip under the broiler if the top needs further browning.

Ratatouille

Recently this hard-to-pronounce French dish became a household word in America overnight, when the delightful movie Ratatouille *swept the country and won our hearts. Not many Americans would begin to know how to make a ratatouille, but that such a dish had the power to evoke an overwhelming taste memory was something we could relate to. I fell in love with ratatouille when I was a* jeune fille *living in Paris, and I have been partial to it ever since. There is a classic way to make it—cooking each of the ingredients separately, then putting them all together—but that is time-consuming, and I'm not really sure that it produces such a superior dish. I feel that rules are made to be bent in cooking, and that there's no harm in simplifying and putting your own imprint on a dish. So here is my version, subject to variations according to the season. I always make triple the amount I'm going to eat immediately, because I put it to so many good uses.*

WHAT YOU NEED

1 medium onion	½ large red bell pepper
¼ cup olive oil	Salt
1 medium eggplant (1 pound or a little more)	2 or 3 medium tomatoes
1 small zucchini	A scattering of chopped fresh parsley

Peel and cut the onion in half lengthwise, then into fairly thick slices. Heat 2 tablespoons of the oil in a large, heavy skillet, and sauté the onion. With a vegetable peeler, partially peel the eggplant, then cut it into even-sized chunks, about ¾ inch each, with a little skin. Cut the zucchini into ¾-inch pieces, too, and toss these vegetables in with the onions and sauté together, stirring frequently. As they brown and the pan gets dry, pour in the remaining olive oil and add the pepper, cut into pieces of the same size. Salt everything, and let cook, covered, for 10 minutes, stirring occasionally. Roughly chop the tomatoes, add them to the skillet, and cook slowly another 10–15 minutes, covered, until everything is tender and intermingled. Taste, and add salt if needed. Sprinkle chopped parsley on top.

Variations

You can include mushrooms—whole, if small, or quartered—adding them when you put in the pepper. You can omit the pepper, but I like the touch of color and the sweetness it adds. You can also include chopped garlic when you're browning the eggplant, but be careful it doesn't brown too much or its flavor will overwhelm.

Second Rounds

Ratatouille is a treasure to have on hand. It is delicious chilled, and wonderful with eggs—in an omelet or with a poached egg embedded in it—and you can use it as a sauce for pasta. For that you'll need ¾–1 cup ratatouille, warmed up and thinned with a little pasta water; this is enough to dress 2–3 ounces of pasta (penne, fusilli, or shells preferred), tossed with more chopped parsley and, of course, with freshly grated Parmesan.

Purée of Parsnips (or Celery Root) and Potatoes

Either of these flavorful, earthy root vegetables blends with potatoes to make a beautiful accompaniment to so many saucy dishes. And what could be simpler? You cook the two together and mash them with a little butter and cream, and they're ready.

WHAT YOU NEED

1 large parsnip, or an equivalent-sized portion of a large celery root

1 equal-sized mealy baking potato*

Salt

2 teaspoons butter

A little heavy cream

*Baking potatoes, such as the russet, are best for mashing, but they are apt to be so huge when you buy them individually that you'll probably use only half. Since you want equal amounts of root vegetable and potato for this purée, just remove the additional potato after you've boiled it and use for another purpose. Or make more of the dish than you need, and create a lovely soup with the leftovers.

Peel the parsnip or celery root, and cut it into large chunks. Do the same with the potato. Boil both in lightly salted water to cover until tender. Drain (and remove, if necessary, excess potato). Mash the root vegetable and potato together in the cooking pot, using either a hand masher or an immersion blender. Add salt, butter, and cream to your liking.

A Potato Dish for Julia

Once, when I was in Cambridge working all day nonstop with Julia Child, as we often did, it was almost 11 p.m. when she finally swept away the manuscript and announced we'd make dinner. She then turned to me and said: "Judith, you make a nice little potato dish while I fix the meat." Slightly unnerved, I managed to rise to the occasion and put together what I would call a fast stove-top version of the classic potatoes Anna. As I mashed some garlic and salt together and smeared this between the layers of sliced potatoes, Julia was looking on a bit skeptically, and although I used lots of butter, of which she always approved, it wasn't clarified butter. But when we sat down and she took her first bite, she pronounced the potatoes delicious, and her husband, Paul, toasted me. I was in cook's heaven.

I probably made my potato dish that night in a standard round 5- or 6-inch skillet for the three of us, but in recent years I've made it regularly for myself in a 4½-inch-square cast-iron frying pan, which once belonged to my father. After he retired, he liked cooking for himself, and I remember his acquiring this little pan with pride so that he could make himself one perfect fried egg. It's unlikely that you'll have such a pan, particularly one imbued with fond memories, but any very small skillet will do.

WHAT YOU NEED

2 medium new potatoes	4 teaspoons butter
1 small garlic clove	Freshly ground pepper
Salt	

Peel the potatoes, and slice them very thin. Peel and mince the garlic, then, with the flat of your chef's knife, mash it with a little salt until it is a paste. Work a little of the butter into it. Heat 2 teaspoons of the butter in your small frying pan over medium-low heat, and lay in half the potato slices, overlapping slightly, to fill the bottom of the pan. Salt and pepper

them lightly, and smear the garlic paste on top. Add the remaining layer of potatoes, and cook gently, setting a small cover askew on top of the pan. After about 8 minutes, turn the potatoes, which should be brown on the bottom, by setting a small, sturdy plate on top of the pan and flipping the potatoes over onto it. They won't hold together in perfect shape, but don't worry. After heating the remaining butter in the pan, just slide the potatoes back in and arrange them as neatly as you can. Let them cook, semi-covered, for about 5 minutes, and uncovered for a couple more minutes, at which point they should be done and nicely browned, both top and bottom. Turn them onto a warm dinner plate, and let them mingle with whatever juicy meat you are having for dinner.

Duxelles: A Way of Preserving Your Mushrooms

When you have bought more mushrooms than you are going to use up in the week ahead, a simple way to keep them is to dice and sauté them, what the French call duxelles. You can then pack the sautéed dice in a small freezer bag and dip into it whenever you want a tablespoon or so to add to a sauce, a soup, an omelet, whatever.

WHAT YOU NEED

¼ pound mushrooms

¼ teaspoon salt

2 teaspoons butter

1 teaspoon vegetable oil

1 shallot, finely chopped

Trim off, if necessary, the woody part of the mushroom stems, and with a damp cloth wipe off any dirt (don't immerse the mushrooms in water). Chop both stems and caps into small dice. Spread them out on a towel, and sprinkle the salt over them. After about 10 minutes, pat dry to remove excess juice. Meanwhile, heat the butter and oil in a fairly large skillet, toss in the shallot, and sauté it gently for about 2 minutes. When the mushrooms have released their liquid, add them to the shallot, and cook together few minutes, until the pan is dry. Cool, and store in the refrigerator for a few days or freeze.

If you want to make up a large batch so you'll always have this treasure at hand to give an intense mushroom flavor, just multiply the above ingredients, and be sure to use a larger pan for the increased amount.

Braised Endive with Ham and Cheese

Endive is an overlooked vegetable in America—at least, few people cook it. But it makes a very special lunch or supper dish when done this way.

WHAT YOU NEED

1 good-sized endive

1 teaspoon butter

1 lemon

Salt

2 thin slices ham or prosciutto

3–4 tablespoons grated cheese (a French mountain cheese such as Cantal, Swiss Gruyère, or Parmigiano-Reggiano)

Cut the endive in half lengthwise. Rub a little of the butter in a heavy skillet just big enough to hold the two halves of endive, then lay them into the pan, side by side. Distribute the remaining butter on top, sprinkle on several drops of lemon juice, and salt lightly. Pour enough boiling water into the pan to come halfway up the endive. Arrange on top a round of parchment cut to fit snugly into the pan, and cover with a tight-fitting lid. Cook over low heat for 30 minutes, at which point check for tenderness: if the endive is soft, finish cooking uncovered until the remaining liquid is absorbed; if it's still resistant, cook covered a little longer, adding more water if needed. When the endive is done, drape a thin slice of ham or prosciutto over each endive half, and sprinkle cheese liberally on top. Slip under a broiler until lightly browned and bubbly. Good with a Wild Rice Pancake (page 180), broiled polenta (page 194), or just a hunk of crusty bread.

Roasted Asparagus with a Sesame Vinaigrette

I learned to roast my asparagus from Nina Simonds, the expert on health-giving Asian foods, and after trying it the first time, I've never turned back. I buy a full ½ pound and extract about four spears before roasting, to save for a stir-fry. Leftovers make a wonderful BLA (see below) or just a salad.

WHAT YOU NEED

½ pound asparagus

½ teaspoon toasted sesame oil

½ teaspoon olive oil

Pinch of salt

SESAME VINAIGRETTE

1 scant tablespoon soy sauce

2 teaspoons rice vinegar

½ teaspoon toasted sesame oil

¾ teaspoon sugar

Trim the tough ends off the asparagus. Lay the spears on a baking tray lined with aluminum foil or Silpat, and drizzle the sesame and olive oils over. Salt lightly. Roll the spears over to coat all sides. Put the pan in a pre-heated 475° oven, and roast the asparagus for 12 minutes. Meanwhile, prepare the vinaigrette, and when the asparagus is done, pour some of it over the spears.

Second Round

BLA (BACON, LETTUCE, AND ASPARAGUS SANDWICH)

If you have leftover asparagus, try making what, according to the food writer David Nussbaum, the natives in Massachusetts—in the Connecticut River Valley, where asparagus is grown—call a BLA: a bacon, lettuce, and asparagus sandwich with mayonnaise. It's delicious.

CELERY ROOT

Celery roots are apt to be large, and with their tough skins, they look forbidding—not a good investment for the single cook, one would think. But when I discovered how roasting thick slices transformed their flavor into something wonderfully earthy and complex, it was a revelation. So now, during the winter months, I often bring home a big celery root. I'll use about half of it for roasting, and the other half I'll make into *céleri rémoulade,* that bistro standby of julienned raw celery root swathed in a mustardy mayonnaise.

ROASTED CELERY ROOT (CELERIAC)

WHAT YOU NEED

1 celery root	Kosher salt
Light olive oil	

Cut the celery root in half, and peel off all the skin from the half you are going to use right away. Cut that portion into pieces about ⅓ inch thick. Rub both sides with a little oil, and sprinkle salt over them. Arrange on a baking sheet (or around roasting meat or poultry), and roast in a preheated 375° oven for about 45 minutes, turning them over once.

CELERY RÉMOULADE

To simulate the classic *céleri rémoulade,* peel the remaining half of your celery root, and cut it with a big sharp knife into very thin sticks. Or use a little hand-cranked machine to shred it, or a food processor, using the fine-shredding blade. For about 3 cups celery root, mix together about ¼ cup mayonnaise (homemade is of course always best, but not necessary), 2 teaspoons Dijon mustard, and 2 tablespoons whole-milk yogurt. Toss in the julienned celery root, and mix well with a couple of tablespoons of chopped parsley. Season with salt and pepper and a little lemon juice, if you think it needs more acidity. This makes an ample amount so you'll have some on hand.

Other Good Roasted Vegetables

It is very convenient when you are roasting a chicken or a piece of meat or fish to roast some compatible vegetables alongside, such as onions and carrots and maybe celery. But it is also rewarding to do a tray full of different vegetables that you are not as apt to roast so what you don't eat right away you can have on hand for salads and cold plates, or to mix with pasta, grains, rice, or eggs. Here are some vegetables that I find particularly handy and delicious when roasted:

BEETS

Trim off the greens, not too close, and wrap whole beets, unpeeled, in foil. Or put them in a small ceramic dish with a cover. Roast small beets at 400° for 35–40 minutes; 1 hour for large beets. Pierce with a skewer or the point of a small knife to make sure they are tender. Peel when cool enough to handle.

EGGPLANT

Partially peel and cut into ½-inch slices. Rub both sides with a little olive oil and salt. Roast small eggplant slices at 400° for 40 minutes; large ones for 50 minutes. To roast whole eggplants, prick all over and roast in a 450° oven for 35–40 minutes, or until soft. When cool enough to handle, cut in half and scrape the flesh into a colander. Chop and use for a salad or for an appetizer dip with a little garlic, salt, sesame paste, lemon, and olive oil.

FENNEL

Remove the tough outer leaves and cut the fennel bulb from stem end to root in ½-inch slices. Rub with a little olive oil and salt and roast at 375° for 30–35 minutes.

GARLIC

Slice off the stem of the whole head, exposing a little of the flesh of the cloves, and drizzle olive oil over. Wrap in foil, or, better still, if you have a small ceramic baking dish with a cover made just for this purpose, use the dish. Roast the head at 375° for 1½ hours. When you want to use the roasted garlic, squeeze out as much of it from the cloves as you wish. It gives a lovely, mild, garlicky butter taste to so many dishes.

LEEK

Trim the root end of the leek and slice off the green leaves. Wash carefully and dry, then roll in a little olive oil. Leave whole and roast for 25–35 minutes, depending on size, at 375°. Prick to see when tender.

MUSHROOMS

Rub large mushrooms caps (saving the stems for soup) or whole medium and small mushrooms with olive oil and roast at 375° for 10–15 minutes. Wild mushrooms can be delicious roasted for 10–20 minutes at 375°, but make sure they are young ones, not old and woody.

ONIONS

Roast small onions, peeled and left whole, for 60 minutes in a 375° oven; shallots will take only about 30 minutes. Large sweet onions, peeled and cut into ⅓-inch rings, then rubbed in olive oil, need 40–45 minutes at 375°.

PARSNIPS

Peel and split large parsnips in half lengthwise (leave whole smaller parsnips and the thin end of large ones), rub with a little olive oil, and roast at 375° for 50 minutes.

PEPPERS

Cut large bell peppers into quarters. Remove ribs and seeds, rub with olive oil, and roast at 425° for 20 minutes. Peel off the charred skin. For an alternative, see the stovetop method, page 242.

POTATOES

Roast small new potatoes, peeled and left whole, at 375° for 60 minutes. Roast large potatoes, peeled and sliced into ¾-inch pieces, at 375° for 45 minutes. Sweet potatoes should be peeled and cut into ½-inch slices. They need about 30 minutes at 375°.

SQUASH, SUMMER

Squash, such as zucchini or yellow squash, can either be cut into 1-inch slices or split lengthwise. Leave unpeeled, rub with a little olive oil, garlic, and salt, and roast at 375° for 20 minutes.

SQUASH, WINTER

Winter squash, such as butternut or acorn or kabuki, should be peeled, cut into 1-inch chunks, and roasted at 375° for 55–60 minutes. Or you can cut the squash in half, rub the inside with butter and roast 1 hour or longer.

TOMATOES

Cut medium to large tomatoes in half and roast at 375° for 45 minutes. Cherry tomatoes tossed in a little olive oil are good roasted for about 10 minutes at 425°. Just experiment with various heirloom types.

TURNIPS

I prefer white turnips, peeled and cut into ⅓-inch slices, rubbed with a little olive oil and salt, and roasted at 375° for 45 minutes.

If you are doing any of the above vegetables alongside a roast, you'll have to adjust your oven temperature according to what the roast requires. So just give the vegetables a little more or a little less time.

I tasted some particularly flavorful roasted vegetables at Nina Simond's table recently, and she told me that she sprinkled a little balsamic vinegar over some of them before roasting. I found that particularly good with asparagus, onions, fennel, and zucchini.

Stir-Fried Vegetables

Stir-frying a combination of vegetables quickly in a small wok gives them a more intense flavor and a pleasing texture, and they benefit from being cooked together. It's a good way to use small amounts of vegetables you may have stored away. You can mix and match as you wish, aiming for good color and flavor complements. You can even poach an egg on top of your stir-fry (see page 105).

WHAT YOU NEED

A green vegetable, such as a small
  zucchini or handful of snow
  peas
1 small carrot
2 or 3 scallions

2 teaspoons light olive oil
1 slice ginger about the size of a
  quarter, peeled
Salt

Cut the zucchini into sticks (or string the snow peas and halve them on the diagonal). Peel the carrot, and cut into fine julienne pieces. Trim the scallions, and slice them in thirds. Heat the oil in a small wok, and toss in the ginger. When it starts to sizzle, pile in the zucchini and carrot, and stir-fry them over high heat for about 30 seconds. Add the scallions, and then a splash or two of water. Turn the heat down to medium, salt to taste, cover, and cook for 1 minute. Uncover, and stir-fry until the vegetables have absorbed all the water and are done to your liking. Eat right away.

Variations

The possibilities are endless. Let yourself be inspired by the season—in spring, for instance, try asparagus, wild leeks, dandelion greens, and young spinach, then vary through summer and fall. As Ed Giobbi often said, "What grows together goes together." You can also use garlic, letting a few slices sizzle along with the ginger; this is particularly good if you're cooking more strong-flavored, assertive vegetables.

Chicken Salad

It's hard to beat a good chicken salad, and it is open to variations, so you need not get tired of it. I prefer a chicken salad that isn't smothered in so much mayonnaise that you can't taste much else, so I tend to go easy on the mayo and temper it with a little yogurt. But play with the dressing to suit your own taste.

WHAT YOU NEED

Leftover cooked chicken, cut into smallish chunks, about 1 cup
1 tablespoon vinaigrette (see variation page 149), preferably made with balsamic vinegar
1 rib tender celery, chopped
1 scallion, finely chopped
¼ bell pepper (red, orange, or green, or a combination), chopped

1 teaspoon drained capers
Chopped fresh parsley, and other fresh herbs if available (tarragon, basil, or marjoram)
Salt and freshly ground pepper
1 teaspoon plain whole-milk yogurt
1½–2 tablespoons mayonnaise
Lettuce leaves or other salad greens

Toss the chicken in a bowl with the vinaigrette, and let stand for 5 minutes or so. Mix in the celery, scallion, bell pepper, capers, and herbs. Season with salt and pepper. Stir the yogurt into the mayonnaise, and fold into the salad. Arrange on a salad plate atop a lettuce leaf or other salad greens.

Variations

There are many good things you can add to this salad, according to your taste and what's around. Toasted walnuts or almonds add crunch, flavor, and substance; other colorful seasonal vegetables, such as pieces of lightly cooked asparagus, snow peas, fava beans, broccoli florets, and artichoke hearts are all welcome. My mother used to garnish her chicken salad with green grapes, each one meticulously peeled and halved.

Asian-Accented Chicken Salad

Here is a good way to use up leftover chicken that makes a full, satisfying meal.

WHAT YOU NEED

Salt

⅓ cup pasta shells or fettuccine

¾–1 cup cooked chicken cut into matchsticks or shredded

A generous tablespoon mayonnaise

2 scallions, sliced

2 small mushrooms, sliced

¼ red bell pepper (or orange or yellow), chopped or julienned

DRESSING

½ teaspoon dry mustard

1 teaspoon sugar

2 teaspoons soy sauce

1 tablespoon toasted sesame oil

2 tablespoons vinegar, preferably white-wine vinegar

GARNISH

A sprinkling of chopped fresh cilantro or parsley

A few lettuce leaves, or some watercress

Bring a pot of salted water to a boil, and toss in the pasta. Cook for about 8 minutes, and then taste; when done al dente, drain. Toss the pasta with the chicken, salt lightly, and fold in the mayonnaise. Let macerate for a few minutes while you make the dressing. Put all the dressing ingredients in a small jar, cover, and shake well to blend. Fold the scallions, mushrooms, and pepper into the chicken, and add about 2½ tablespoons of the dressing. Toss to blend, then taste, and add more dressing as you see fit. Sprinkle cilantro or parsley on top, and surround the salad with a few greens.

Variations

Try adding a quarter of an avocado, peeled and chopped, or a few cooked artichoke hearts, and/or some small, sweet cherry tomatoes, split in half. You could also substitute some lightly cooked broccoli florets or broccolini, or asparagus—whatever is in season and handy.

Use leftover white turkey meat if you have it, instead of chicken.

Second Round

You'll eat up all the salad, I promise. But you'll have some dressing left, and it's good on so many things—fish, hot or chilled; warm noodles; and almost any green vegetable—you'll be glad to have it as a standby (double or triple the amount if you want).

Preserving an Avocado

The single cook is apt to resist buying an avocado because any leftover portion turns brown so quickly when refrigerated. But if you keep the uneaten part intact—that is, leave the skin on and the pit in place— and rub the cut surface with lemon juice, then wrap the piece tightly in plastic wrap, it will keep for several days in the fridge. And a nice ripe avocado always adds interesting flavor and texture, so don't deny yourself.

Vinaigrette

It is so easy to make a vinaigrette, the classic French salad dressing, that I can't fathom why so many people living alone go out and buy bottled dressings. Not only do they pay more, but the dressing never tastes as fresh, and you can't vary the seasonings as you wish. So I beg you to make your own vinaigrette as part of your cooking life. The amounts I'm giving will be enough to dress two or three small salads, but you can double or triple the quantities if you're an avid salad consumer and want enough dressing to see you through the week. Just refrigerate the extra in a jar, tightly sealed.

WHAT YOU NEED

¼ teaspoon salt

¼ teaspoon Dijon mustard

1 tablespoon red-wine vinegar

3 tablespoons extra-virgin olive oil

Put the salt, mustard, and vinegar in a small jar (I find an empty Dijon-mustard jar a good size), and shake it to dissolve the salt. Pour in the olive oil, and shake again thoroughly. Now taste, and adjust the seasonings to your liking. Pour about 1 tablespoon over your salad, toss thoroughly, and taste again to determine how much more you want to add.

Variations and Additions

- Try using fresh lemon juice instead of vinegar to vary the flavor, starting with 2 teaspoons and adding more after you've tasted. The lemon accent is particularly pleasant with young greens, but I prefer a good wine vinegar for everyday use.
- White-wine vinegar, champagne vinegar, and occasionally a good balsamic are all welcome for a change.
- Add a small, finely chopped shallot (or a portion of a large one) to the vinaigrette, and shake well. Or, if you want a more assertive

dressing, mash a small clove of garlic with a little salt, and shake that up with the dressing. It is better to add both shallots and garlic shortly before dressing the salad, because they don't keep well in the dressing, even if it's refrigerated.

- The same goes for herbs; if you want to add a little fresh tarragon or basil or dill, do it just before dressing.

Some cooks prefer to make their dressing in a salad bowl, then plop the greens on top and toss. But I find that you are less in control, not knowing how much dressing you'll need for the amount of greens you'll be using. Better to use the Italian method, which is to salt the salad lightly, then slowly pour on enough olive oil to lightly coat the greens, and finally sprinkle on just enough vinegar to add the zest—all the time tossing and tasting.

Blue Cheese Dressing

1 ½ tablespoons yogurt

1 ½ tablespoons mashed blue
   cheese

1 tablespoon olive oil

2 teaspoons white-wine vinegar
   or rice vinegar

3 or 4 drops of honey (about
   ⅛ teaspoon)

Salt to taste

Mix everything together in a small bottle, cover tightly, and shake until it is well mixed. Taste, and adjust the seasonings to your liking; it may need a little salt, but not much. This makes enough for at least two individual salads. It's particularly good with the Roasted Beet, Arugula, and Endive Salad (page 152), and can be delicious just spooned over a chilled vegetable.

Salad Greens—Keeping Them Fresh

It's handy to be able to buy a variety of salad greens to last the week, but you want them to remain fresh. I have found that the best solution is to store them in one of those large plastic domes (mine is about 8 inches in diameter and the same in height, with a 3-quart capacity). I wash the greens first, spin them dry very thoroughly, shake them out a bit, pile them loosely in the bowl of the dome, and slap on its tight cover. This way they can breathe rather than being smothered in a plastic bag. And you can buy a variety, so that you're not eating the same old lettuce all week. I like a small mix of baby greens (not a whole package) and something crisp, such as romaine, and something assertive, such as arugula, to say nothing of that bitter touch that endive, frisée, and radicchio give you. Watercress is also a good choice, but only when it's fresh-looking, and I love the purslane that grows wild in my garden in the summer.* So try to change your selection a little each week and find new combinations.

*Purslane is often considered a weed. It grows prolifically in my northern Vermont garden, and I would have just plucked it out if I hadn't heeded the words of Ed Giobbi, the gifted cook and painter—and gardener. He told me never to weed too vigorously, because there may always be hidden, beneath the useless weeds, small plants like purslane and wild sorrel that are treasures. And that's how I found purslane, which crawls along the ground, sending out small, fleshy, almost round leaves that are just a little peppery and add great taste and texture to a salad. They're also good stir-fried if you have a sufficient crop (certainly you'll find enough for one serving).

Roasted Beet, Arugula, and Endive Salad with Blue Cheese Dressing

1 medium roasted beet (see page 142)

A handful of arugula leaves, torn

Several endive leaves, halved crosswise

A sprinkling of pumpkin or sunflower seeds

About 2 tablespoons Blue Cheese Dressing (page 150)

Peel the beet, and cut it into matchstick pieces. Toss these in an individual salad or soup bowl with the arugula, endive, and seeds. Pour the dressing on, and toss all together.

Fennel, Apple, and Walnut Salad

Here's a sparkling salad that makes superb use of that one-third or so of a plump fennel bulb that you couldn't consume in one sitting.

WHAT YOU NEED

Fennel, about ⅓ medium bulb or ½ small one

½ tart apple

About 6 walnuts

DRESSING

¼ teaspoon Dijon mustard

Pinch of salt

1 teaspoon fresh lemon juice, or more to taste

½ teaspoon balsamic vinegar

1 tablespoon olive oil, or more to taste

Remove the course outside rib of the fennel bulb, and trim off the stalk, saving the leaves. Trim the root end so the bulb stands firmly, and with a

Fennel, Apple, and Walnut Salad continued

sharp knife cut *very thin* slices. If you have a mandoline, by all means use it. Core the apple, and cut it into thin slices, leaving the peel on. Mix together the dressing ingredients, taste, and adjust as you see fit. Pour the dressing over the fennel and apple slices with the walnuts, broken in half, and some of the fennel leaves chopped, and toss everything together. Pile onto a salad plate, and top with a few more fennel leaves.

Tabbouleh

This nourishing bulgur-wheat salad provides a satisfying way of using up some of the huge bunch of parsley that the supermarket foisted on you. If it's wintertime and you don't have access to fresh mint, use ½ teaspoon dried mint and stir it into the still-warm bulgur after you've drained it, so the mint will have a chance to expand and release its flavor.

WHAT YOU NEED

Salt

⅓ cup bulgur wheat

¼ cup chopped fresh mint, or ½ teaspoon dried mint (see headnote)

Freshly ground pepper

1 small-to-medium sweet ripe tomato, chopped

2 or 3 scallions, chopped

½ cup chopped fresh parsley

DRESSING

¼ cup lemon juice

¼ cup olive oil

Large pinch of salt

GARNISH

Purslane, watercress, or lettuce

Bring ⅔ cup water to a boil with a pinch of salt. Toss the bulgur in a bowl, and pour the boiling water over it. Cover, and let stand for 30 minutes. Drain the bulgur, pressing it in the strainer to extract the water. If you're using dried mint, stir it into the warm bulgur now. After 30 minutes, season with salt and pepper, and add the tomato, scallions, parsley, and fresh mint, if using. Whisk the lemon juice and olive oil together in a small bowl, and add salt to taste. Pour the dressing over the tabbouleh, and toss everything together. Spoon onto a salad plate, and surround with purslane, if you can find it, or other leaves.

Warm Potato Salad with Sausage

One of my favorite suppers is a good sausage with warm potato salad. I love the way the sausage juices mingle with the tender new potatoes bathed in a mustardy vinaigrette—a very French taste that makes me nostalgic.

WHAT YOU NEED

2 or 3 new potatoes

1 or 2 large sausages, such as sweet Italian, Polish kielbasa, chorizo, or hard-to-find French garlic sausage

2 teaspoons oil

A splash of red wine

DRESSING

1 teaspoon Dijon mustard

A good pinch of salt

1 tablespoon red-wine vinegar

2 tablespoons olive oil

3 scallions, sliced

2 or 3 fresh sprigs parsley, chopped

Boil the potatoes in a small pot with plenty of water for about 20 minutes, or until tender. After about 10 minutes, prick the sausages and put them in a small skillet that you've rubbed with oil. Brown on both sides, and cook slowly, turning occasionally, for a total of about 20 minutes. Meanwhile, make the dressing by mixing all the dressing ingredients in a bowl. When the potatoes are ready, drain them and cut them into fairly thick slices (no need to peel them, unless you prefer to). Toss the warm potatoes with the vinaigrette. At this point, the sausages should be ready. Remove them to a plate, and add a splash of red wine to the pan, cooking it down quickly until it is syrupy. Pour this bit of pan juice over however much of the sausage you plan to eat right away, and serve it to yourself with the warm potato salad.

Second Round

I've deliberately called for more sausage here than I would eat in one sitting, because I like to have some cooked sausage in the fridge to use in a frittata or an omelet or a hearty soup, or to add to a pasta sauce. It's very handy. So determine for yourself how much sausage you want to cook.

Fish Salad

You can use almost any kind of leftover fish in this salad.

WHAT YOU NEED

1 teaspoon lemon juice

Pinch of salt

1 tablespoon olive oil

½ shallot, or 1 scallion, finely chopped

2 teaspoons chopped fresh dill or tarragon or, if not available, parsley

A piece of cooked fish, flaked or cut into bite-sized pieces, about ¾ cup

¼ cup mayonnaise, preferably homemade (page 111)

2 teaspoons capers, rinsed and patted dry

Watercress or young salad greens

1 hard-boiled egg (see page 107), sliced

Whisk together in a bowl the lemon juice, salt, olive oil, shallot or scallion, and half of the fresh herbs. Add the fish. Let marinate, turning once or twice, for about 20 minutes. Fold in the mayonnaise and half the capers. Make a bed of watercress or salad greens on a plate, pile the fish salad on top, arrange the hard-boiled egg slices around, and sprinkle the remaining herbs and capers on top.

Variation

This could also be made with smoked salmon, tossed with slices of avocado, cucumbers, or asparagus.

Pesto

This is a sauce to have on hand at all times. It keeps well in the refrigerator for at least a week if you film the top of it with olive oil (and refilm after you have dipped into it and taken some from the jar), and it keeps its bloom for a couple of months frozen. It's a good idea to freeze it in an ice tray, and then store the cubes in plastic storage bags. That way, you easily can get at just the amount you need.

WHAT YOU NEED

3 fat garlic cloves

1 teaspoon salt

4 cups loosely packed basil leaves

2 tablespoons toasted pine nuts

½ cup extra-virgin olive oil, plus a little more to film the top

I like to smash the garlic, slip off the peels, and mash the cloves with salt with a mortar and pestle. I scrape that out into a food processor, add the basil and pine nuts, and process to a paste, scraping down the sides. This method seems to mash the garlic more thoroughly, but you can just dump everything into the food processor and let it do the work. Slowly add ½ cup of the olive oil, and process until well blended. Transfer the pesto to a small jar, and pour the remaining olive oil on top.

Variations

If you are using the pesto as a light sauce to dress cold meats, fish, or poultry, you may want to hold back on the pine nuts. But add them when you want to dress a pasta. For that, all you need is a big pot of salted boiling water and 2 or 3 ounces of spaghetti or other pasta. When the pasta is al dente, drain and toss with about ¼ cup of pesto and lots of grated Parmesan. Season, of course, to taste.

Because mint grows so much more abundantly than basil in northern Vermont, I've tried adding mint to my pesto, following Ed Giobbi's advice, and it gives it a slightly different, pleasant kick. Add about ¾ cup mint to the above ingredients, and you might include an additional garlic clove.

Winter Green Sauce

This is a good way to make use of those unnecessarily large bouquets of parsley that we get at our supermarkets, as well as fennel fronds that usually go to waste.

WHAT YOU NEED

3 scallions, chopped
Fennel leaves, roughly chopped, enough to make about ¼ cup
Parsley leaves, roughly chopped, enough to make about 1 cup
1 garlic clove
Salt
¼ cup light olive oil
¼ lemon

Put the scallions, fennel leaves, and parsley in the bowl of a food processor or a mini-chopper, and process until finely chopped. Smash the garlic clove, peel it, and chop the flesh. Sprinkle on about ¼ teaspoon salt, and mash it with the garlic, using the flat of a big knife, smearing it back and

Winter Green Sauce continued

forth until you have a paste. Or this can be done with a mortar and pestle. (In fact, the whole sauce can be made with a mortar and pestle—good exercise for your upper-arm muscles, Julia Child would say.)

Back to the food processor: Scrape the garlic paste in, and pour in almost all the olive oil and most of the juice of the quarter-lemon. Process again until almost puréed, scraping down the sides as necessary. Stop and taste. Add more salt and a few more drops of lemon juice, if you think they are needed. Transfer the sauce to a small jar, scraping it all out with a rubber spatula, and float the remaining olive oil on top. Refrigerate, and use within a week; otherwise, freeze. If you're using just a few tablespoons, float more olive oil on top before refrigerating again, to help preserve the color and freshness.

Sauce Gribiche

I prefer this sauce to any other for cold meats, fish, and poultry, or those innards that I like so much.

WHAT YOU NEED

½ teaspoon salt

1 tablespoon red-wine vinegar

1 tablespoon olive oil

1 tablespoon drained capers

2 cornichons, chopped into small pieces, or, if unavailable, use about 1 tablespoon chopped dill pickle

1 hard-boiled egg (see page 107), chopped fine

Freshly ground pepper to taste

1 tablespoon chopped fresh parsley

Mix all the ingredients together. If you are not using all the sauce right away, hold back the parsley, and add just before serving. Be sure to taste after you've mixed everything, and adjust the seasonings to your liking.

Ed Giobbi's Fresh Mint Sauce

I have lots of mint in my herb garden in the summer, and I love to make this sauce, which is good on so many things. Ed recommends it for vegetables, poultry, meats (particularly lamb), and fish.

WHAT YOU NEED

2 cups fresh mint leaves
2 sprigs fresh parsley, leaves
   chopped
¼ cup pine nuts
4 garlic cloves, peeled and
   chopped

¼ cup extra-virgin olive oil
¼ cup chicken broth
Salt and freshly ground pepper

Purée all the ingredients in the food processor, using just a pinch of salt. Taste, and add more salt and pepper to your liking. Process again until the sauce is the consistency of heavy cream.

Tomato Sauce

There's nothing like knowing you have stashed away in your freezer good tomato sauce made from sweet San Marzano canned tomatoes. It comes in handy in so many ways. I usually make 3 cups of thick sauce, to freeze in 1-cup containers. You can easily double or triple that amount if you're feeling ambitious and have enough freezer space.

WHAT YOU NEED

1 tablespoon olive oil

1 medium onion, chopped

2 garlic cloves, peeled and slivered

One 28-ounce can tomatoes, preferably San Marzano

A sprig of fresh basil leaves, if available

A good pinch of salt

Heat the oil in a heavy medium pot, and sauté the onion until it begins to soften. Add the garlic, and sauté another minute or two; don't let it brown. Pour in the tomatoes, squishing them with your hands. Pour a cup of water into the can, and swirl it around to get up the remaining tomatoes, and then pour that into the sauce. Stir, bring to a boil, drop in the basil, and sprinkle salt over it. Cook at a lively simmer, stirring occasionally and scraping up the tomatoes from the bottom of the pan, adding a little more water if the sauce is getting too thick. I like my sauce thick for storage. I can always add broth and/or water or pasta water to thin it later.

Cucumber Raita

This is an Indian sauce introduced to me by Madhur Jaffrey years ago, and I have been making it steadily ever since. It is, of course, good with almost any Indian curry dish, and I find that it is also delicious with cold chicken, lamb, salmon, or shrimp—in other words, an excellent way of dressing up leftovers.

WHAT YOU NEED

1 small cucumber (no more than 4 inches long;), peeled*

Salt

¾–1 cup whole-milk yogurt

Pinch of cayenne (optional)

A sprinkling of cumin seed

A light dusting of paprika

Grate the cucumber, and sprinkle a little salt on top. Put the yogurt in a bowl, starting with ¾ cup, and beat until smooth. Pat the cucumber dry with a paper towel, and mix in with the yogurt. Add a small pinch of cayenne, if using (I like it without if I am eating this with something highly seasoned), and more salt to taste. Sprinkle cumin and a light dusting of paprika on top.

*A pickling cucumber can be used, or just a small garden variety of cucumber. If neither of those is available, try the slim Persian kind (they usually come only in a pack of six, but get someone to share the pack with you).

Cream Sauce

Since this is one of those staples that is nice to have stashed away in your freezer, I am giving proportions for a larger amount of sauce than you'll probably have immediate need for. If you want to make less, just halve the recipe. Trying to make less than that really doesn't work well. And, of course, you can double the recipe.

WHAT YOU NEED

4 tablespoons butter

4 tablespoons all-purpose flour

2½ cups hot milk

Salt and freshly ground pepper

A few gratings of nutmeg

Melt the butter in a small, heavy pot. Add the flour, and cook over low heat, stirring constantly, for about 3 minutes. Do not let the butter begin to brown. This procedure is known as cooking the roux, to eliminate the uncooked flour taste. Now remove the pan from the heat, and let the bubbling die down. Pour all of the milk in, start whisking furiously, and return to a low heat. Continue to whisk until the sauce thickens. When it does, let it gently simmer another 3–4 minutes, stirring occasionally. Season with salt (starting with ½ teaspoon, then taste), plus several grindings of the pepper mill and a few gratings of nutmeg.

Second Round

Pour what you don't use into ½-cup or 1-cup plastic containers, and freeze. Let the sauce come to room temperature slowly, then pour into a small pan and heat slowly, whisking until smooth.

Five Rice, Pasta, Grains, and Legumes

Long-Grain Rice
Basmati Rice
Brown Rice
Mushroom Risotto
A Quick Risotto with Veal, Chestnuts, and Mushrooms
American Fried Rice
A Provençal Tian of Rice and Greens
British Kedgeree
Indian Leftover Rice with Mushrooms
Vegetable Sushi Rice Salad
Wild Rice
Wild Rice Pilaf
Wild Rice Salad
Wild Rice Pancake
Penne with Tuna, Plum Tomatoes, and Black Olives
Fusilli with Mushrooms, Liver, and Cherry Tomatoes
Penne with Broccoli Rabe and Garlic
Linguine with Smoked Salmon Sauce
Spaghettini with Cockles and Mussels, Alive, Alive O!
Pasta Sauces from Leftovers and Freezer Treasures
Lamb, Mushroom, and Barley Casserole
Couscous

Rice, pastas, grains, and legumes (or dried beans) serve both as accompaniments to many of the main-course dishes I give in the first chapter, and also as splendid carriers for the leftovers you are bound to have if you've shopped and cooked with your eye on tomorrow. We are fortunate today in the wide variety of rices, grains, and dried beans we can get. So keep a good selection on hand. With a little effort, you can make them taste delicious. And they're both healthy and easy on your food budget.

RICE

My cooking friends and mentors are usually scornful of the idea that you can successfully cook just ½ cup of rice. But I assure you that you can. All you need is a small, heavy pot (my Le Creuset has a 4-cup capacity, with a bottom diameter of 4½ inches) and a tight-fitting lid. A ½ cup of rice will be more than plenty for one as an accompaniment, but you want to have extra on hand to make any of a number of different cooked rice dishes, or a rice salad (see page 179), or just to thicken a soup. If you want even more, double the amounts.

Long-Grain Rice

WHAT YOU NEED

½ cup long-grain rice

1 cup water

½ teaspoon salt (don't use salt if the rice is to go with an Asian stir-fry)

Put the rice in your small, heavy pot, and pour the cup of water over. Add the salt and bring to a boil. As soon as it boils vigorously, turn the heat way down, so that the rice is simmering very gently. Put the lid on; if you find that it's not really tight-fitting, cover the top first with foil, tucking it around the edges, and then put the lid on. Cook over low heat for 15 minutes. Remove the pot from the heat and let stand for 5 minutes, then fluff up the rice with a fork.

Basmati Rice

Rinse ½ cup basmati rice thoroughly in cold water, rubbing it through your fingers, and drain. Put it in the heavy pot with ¾ cup water and a pinch of salt, bring to a boil, and cook it slowly, covered, for 25 minutes.

Brown Rice

Put ⅔ cup brown rice in a heavy pot, cover with 1⅓ cups water and ½ teaspoon salt, and bring to a boil. Cook slowly, covered, for 1 hour. Check to see that the water hasn't boiled away, and, if necessary, add a bit more as needed.

Risotto

Again, I'm afraid that most of my culinary mentors would take a dim view of the idea of cooking risotto for one. But it can be done very successfully, and if you love risotto, as I do, you'll enjoy every minute of preparing it mindfully. You can make a salad, set the table, watch the news, giving frequent stirs and adding more liquid to the pot, and before you know it the risotto is ready. I do offer on the following page a simplified risotto that requires less attention, so if you've never made a risotto, you may want to start by making that one first.

Mushroom Risotto

¼ cup dried mushrooms, such as porcini, morels, or hen of the woods

½ cup warm water

1¼–1½ cups flavorful broth (chicken, duck, goose, or vegetable stock)

1 tablespoon olive oil

2 fat shallots, chopped

⅔ cup short-grain Italian rice, such as Arborio

A generous splash of white wine

¼ pound fresh mushrooms

1 tablespoon butter

A sprinkling of grated Parmesan

Soak the dried mushrooms in the warm water for 30 minutes. Strain over a small pan to catch the soaking liquid, then pour in the broth, and heat just to a simmer. Meanwhile, heat the oil in a small, heavy pot, and sauté the shallots slowly for 4–5 minutes, until they have released their liquid but are not at all browned. Add the rice, and let it glaze as you stir it— about 1 minute. Pour in the wine, and reduce it until it's absorbed. Now start adding the hot broth liquid about ⅓ cup at a time, stirring and scraping up the rice from the bottom. After each addition of liquid is absorbed, add the next, stirring frequently.

Meanwhile, in another small pan, sauté the fresh mushrooms in 2 teaspoons of the butter. When they have released their liquid, add the drained dried mushrooms and stir together. When the rice has cooked about 20 minutes and has absorbed most of the hot liquid, toss the mushrooms in with the rice. Add the remaining liquid, and let everything cook together for 4–5 minutes. Remove from the heat, and fold in the remaining teaspoon of butter and the Parmesan. Spoon into a warm bowl, and relish every mouthful of this creamy, earthy dish.

A Quick Risotto with Veal, Chestnuts, and Mushrooms

In her most recent book, Lidia Cooks from the Heart of Italy, *the great Italian cook Lidia Bastianich introduces us to various risottos that don't require the patient long cooking and stirring as you pour hot liquid into the rice little by little. In this simpler version, you simply stir the rice into hot chicken broth along with the embellishment ingredients, and when it all comes to a boil, slap on the lid, and cook at a brisk simmer for about 17 minutes. And it's done—a whole delicious and satisfying dinner.*

WHAT YOU NEED

2 teaspoons light olive oil

1 small shallot, minced

3 smallish cremini mushrooms, chopped

3 or 4 chestnuts, chopped

A splash of white wine

½–¾ cup leftover braised veal, cut in small chunks

Salt and freshly ground pepper

⅔ cup chicken broth or water, plus more if needed

⅓ cup short-grain rice, such as Arborio

2 tablespoons grated Parmesan

Heat the oil in a small, heavy pot, and sauté the shallot and mushrooms for about 3 minutes, stirring frequently, until softened. Add the chestnuts,

A Quick Risotto continued

and sauté another minute; then splash in the wine and cook down a little. Add the meat, and salt and pepper to taste, and then pour in the broth. When it comes to a boil, stir in the rice, turn the heat down to a lively simmer, cover, and cook for about 17 minutes. Check and taste. If the rice is just tender and creamy, it is done; if not, add a little more broth and cook another 1–2 minutes. Turn off the heat, and stir in the cheese. Dish up into a warm soup plate.

Variations

This is a recipe to play with and vary according to what cooked meat, poultry, or seafood you may have left over and what vegetables you have on hand.

COOKED RICE DISHES

Every rice-eating country seems to have its share of cooked-rice dishes. Rice is a great carrier, and you need never tire of it, because there are so many different ways of using it that reflect the country of origin. We Americans embrace them all. Here are some that I particularly like.

American Fried Rice

WHAT YOU NEED

1 tablespoon fat (preferably pork or duck fat)
1 small onion, chopped
¼ green bell pepper
½ rib celery, chopped
3 or 4 mushrooms, chopped (optional)

Salt
Dash of hot red-pepper flakes
1 slice country ham, chopped, or ⅓ cup chopped cooked pork
¾–1 cup cooked rice
Soy sauce

Melt the fat in a small-to-medium skillet, and gently fry the onion, green pepper, celery, and mushrooms until softened—5–6 minutes. Salt lightly, and sprinkle on hot pepper to taste. Stir in the ham or pork, the rice, and a generous sprinkling of soy sauce, and let cook until the rice is warmed through and a little crisp on the bottom.

A Provençal Tian of Rice and Greens

"Tian" is a Provençal word for a shallow pottery dish, and there are almost as many tians as there are vegetables. The common ingredient is usually cooked rice enlivened with a green vegetable, aromatic seasonings, and cheese. To make it for one, use a shallow, single-portion baking dish.

WHAT YOU NEED

2 large handfuls of a leafy green vegetable (spinach, Swiss chard, beet greens, turnip greens)
1 tablespoon olive oil
1 garlic clove, peeled and slivered
Salt
¾ cup cooked rice, or more if wanted

1 tablespoon butter
Freshly ground pepper
About 3 tablespoons breadcrumbs
A generous sprinkling of good aged cheese

Rinse the greens and remove and discard really tough stems; if you're using Swiss chard, cut the stems into ½-inch pieces and include. Heat the olive oil in a skillet or a wok, and sizzle the garlic for a few moments, but don't let it turn brown. Dump in the greens with the water still clinging to them, and stir them around. Cook, adding a little more water as needed, and season with salt. When just tender—about 3 minutes for spinach, a bit longer for coarser greens—toss in the rice and half the butter and mix. Taste for seasoning, and add more salt and several turns of the pepper grinder. Transfer the contents to a shallow baking dish, cover lightly with breadcrumbs, and dot with the remaining butter. Sprinkle on enough cheese to cover the top. Bake in a preheated 350° oven for 15 minutes. If you want to brown the top a little more, slip the dish under the broiler.

Variations

A zucchini tian is awfully good, and you don't need to precook the zucchini. Just use a small one, and grate it on the coarse holes of a grater. Salt it and pat dry with a towel, then mix in with the rice. Proceed as above.

If you want to make a more substantial dish, fold in some small lumps of goat cheese or mozzarella and a few slices of shredded ham.

British Kedgeree

Jane Grigson points out in her book English Food *that this dish, borrowed from a Hindu creation of rice and lentils called* khichri, *became a favorite breakfast item among the Brits. However, she warns, it is only as good as the fish that goes into it, so don't use tired leftovers. But good fish that has been recently and carefully prepared (i.e., not overcooked) is fine, and be generous with the butter and the cream. I have made this with salmon, flounder, and red snapper—all good.*

WHAT YOU NEED

1 tablespoon butter
¼ dried hot red pepper
⅔–¾ cup cooked rice
Cooked fish, enough to make
    ½–¾ cup, flaked
Salt
¼ cup heavy cream

½ teaspoon Madras curry
    powder, or more to taste
½ hard-boiled egg (see page
    107), sliced
A sprinkling of chopped fresh
    parsley

Heat the butter in a small, heavy pot, and add the hot pepper. Let it sizzle in the oil and turn dark, then fish it out and discard. Stir the rice and the fish into the pot, salt to taste, and leave over low heat to warm through. Meanwhile, simmer the cream and curry powder together until the cream thickens. Transfer the rice and fish to a warm bowl, pour the curried cream over, and garnish with the hard-boiled egg slices and a scattering of parsley.

Indian Leftover Rice with Mushrooms

This is a recipe adapted from Madhur Jaffrey's first book, An Invitation to Indian Cooking, *written when none of us knew the spices and hot peppers that she introduced us to. It's a simple dish that makes your leftover rice come alive in surprising ways. You can eat it just as is for a light lunch or supper, or as an accompaniment to a Western meat course. I like it alone with some Cucumber Raita (page 163) alongside.*

WHAT YOU NEED

1 tablespoon vegetable oil

About ⅓ medium onion, finely chopped

3 medium mushrooms, chopped into small dice

¼–⅓ hot green chili, thinly sliced

½ teaspoon ground cumin

½ teaspoon ground coriander

⅔ cup cooked rice

2–3 tablespoons chicken or beef broth or water

Salt

A sprinkling of chopped coriander leaves (optional)

Heat the oil in a small skillet, and add the onion. Sauté for a few minutes, then add the mushrooms and continue to sauté, stirring, 3 or 4 minutes. Toss in the sliced chili, and after a minute add the cumin, the coriander, and the rice. Stir vigorously, breaking up any lumps in the rice, and cook over low heat for 5 minutes. If the rice is sticking, add a little broth or water, cover, and cook over low heat for about 5 minutes, adding more broth if necessary. Taste, and add salt to your liking. Spoon the rice onto a warm plate, and sprinkle a little fresh coriander (more commonly known here as cilantro) on top, if available, and if you like it.

Vegetable Sushi Rice Salad

Here's a simple Japanese way with cooked rice that Hiroko Shimbo showed me when I asked her one day what she would do with leftover rice. It's called sushi salad because it's made with sushi rice. As Hiroko points out so persuasively in her book The Sushi Experience, *it's the rice that makes it sushi, not all the various garnishes or tasty bits that are wrapped—or, in this case, tossed—in the seasoned rice. This is one of those dishes that are subject to variations depending on the season, but it's hard to improve on the following intoxicatingly delicious summer version.*

WHAT YOU NEED

1 cup cooked rice*

1½ tablespoons rice vinegar or white-wine vinegar

1 teaspoon sugar

½ teaspoon salt

About ⅓ small zucchini or yellow squash, cut into small dice (⅓ cup)

⅓ cup corn kernels cut from the cob

A strip of a red bell pepper cut into small dice (¼ cup)

1 teaspoon vegetable oil or light olive oil

2 tablespoons minced pickled ginger

*Hiroko, of course, uses short-grain sushi rice, but you can use medium- or even long-grain rice.

The rice should be warm when you mix it with the dressing, so if it is cold from the refrigerator, pour boiling water over it in a strainer or zap it briefly in the microwave. Turn the rice into a bowl (preferably wooden), and break up any lumps. Whisk the vinegar, sugar, and salt together, and pour this dressing over the rice. Mix well. Toss the zucchini, corn, and pepper together with the oil. Heat a skillet or a wok, and when it is hot, stir-fry the vegetables over high heat until they are crisp-cooked, 1–2 minutes. Toss everything together in a serving bowl with the pickled ginger, and eat warm or at room temperature, using chopsticks.

Variation

For a winter salad, Hiroko's vegetables would be cauliflower, string beans, carrots, and perhaps a winter green such as Russian kale.

Wild Rice

Wild rice isn't really a rice—it's a grain—and the best of it comes from Native Americans in the upper Midwest who harvest it in the traditional way, beating the ripened grains into their canoes at harvest time. The cultivated variety is all right and takes a little less time to cook, but it doesn't have the texture of the wild variety. Evan, being a loyal Minnesotan, always sent for wild rice from Blackduck, Minnesota, and I have kept up the tradition, ordering Slindee wild rice, as the producers are now known. It takes about an hour for wild rice to cook, so it's not for a quick dinner. But it reheats perfectly, and I always make extra and enjoy it in a number of ways.

WHAT YOU NEED

¾ cup wild rice
About 3½ cups water or chicken
   broth or a combination of
   water and broth

Large pinch of salt

Rinse the rice in water, rubbing it through your fingertips. Drain, and put it in a small, heavy pot with 3 cups cold water or broth and salt. Bring to a boil, then turn the heat down to a lively simmer. Set the cover askew, and cook, checking and adding more water if needed. After 50 minutes, taste—if the grain is tender and the liquid absorbed, it's done; if not, cook another 5–10 minutes.

Wild Rice Pilaf

WHAT YOU NEED

1 batch cooked Wild Rice
   (preceding recipe)
4 or 5 mushrooms, quartered
About 2 teaspoons butter or light
   olive oil
3 or 4 scallions, cut in half
   lengthwise (if they are very
   thin, leave them whole)

A small handful of snow peas
A scattering of slivered almonds
A couple of slices ham or
   prosciutto, in strips (optional)

If the wild rice you have prepared has cooled, pour boiling water over it to warm it. Sauté the mushrooms in the butter or light olive oil for 3 or 4 minutes. Add the warmed rice, the scallions, and the snow peas to the pot and cook for a minute or two. Correct the seasoning, spoon everything onto a warm plate, and scatter the almonds on top. The addition of ham or prosciutto is only if you want to make a more substantial dish, and you can add the meat during the last minute or so of cooking, just long enough to warm it through.

Variation

Try other vegetables according to the season: asparagus spears, zucchini cut into matchstick-sized pieces, blanched green beans or fava beans, or artichoke hearts.

Wild Rice Salad

¾ cup cooked Wild Rice
(page 177)
Either ¼ cooked Portuguese
chouriço sausage, diced, or
4 or 5 cooked small shrimp,
or both
½ rib celery, chopped

⅛ large red bell pepper, chopped
1 scallion, chopped
2 tablespoons chopped herbs
(parsley, celery leaves, basil,
or tarragon, if available)
Salt and freshly ground pepper

GARNISH
Lettuce leaves
A few black olives

DRESSING
3–4 tablespoons vinaigrette
(page 149)

Toss the salad ingredients together, adding salt and pepper to taste. Pour on the dressing and toss again. Spoon onto a salad plate, and surround with lettuce and black olives.

Variations

Use any cooked rice or grain instead of the wild rice, and vary the ingredients according to your fancy. Chicken, turkey, and ham are all good here, and you can substitute other vegetables, such as asparagus, snap peas, fennel, or small cucumbers.

Wild Rice Pancake

This is apt to be a messy-looking pancake. But who cares? It's just for you, and it's delicious. I particularly like it with a slice or two of smoked salmon and a dollop of sour cream, or of the creamy top of good whole-milk yogurt. But the pancake goes with so many things.

WHAT YOU NEED

⅔–¾ cup cooked wild rice

3 scallions, finely chopped

Salt and freshly ground pepper

2 teaspoons instant-blending flour

1 egg

Vegetable oil

Toss the rice with the scallions and season with salt and pepper to taste. Beat the flour into the egg, and pour it into the wild rice. Mix well. Film the bottom of a large skillet with oil, heat it, and when it is hot, scoop up half the wild-rice batter and plop it into the pan. Quickly flatten the cake out with a spatula. Do the same with the remaining batter. There will be lots of spluttering and popping, so beware. When one side has crisped, turn each cake over with a spatula as best you can, and brown the other side.

I learned from working with Lidia Bastianich the art of making the quick pasta dish: bring a big pot of generously salted water to a boil, plunge in the pasta, and let it cook while you make a sauce. Then, when the pasta is just al dente, transfer it with tongs and a big strainerlike spoon, or spider, to the sauce in its pan, so the two can marry and finish together. It's fast work, and everything serves a purpose, even the salty pasta water when you need to thin your sauce. And it's a perfect way for the home cook to make a balanced, tasty supper for one in no time, using ingredients that are either on the kitchen cupboard shelf, left over in the fridge, or plucked from the garden or a farmers' market stall.

Penne with Tuna, Plum Tomatoes, and Black Olives

WHAT YOU NEED

Salt

2–3 ounces penne, according to appetite (fusilli or small shells are good, too)

1 tablespoon olive oil

1 small onion or fat shallot, sliced thin

1 garlic clove, peeled and sliced thin

2 or 3 ripe plum tomatoes, cut into rough chunks

A splash of white wine

2½–3 ounces canned tuna in olive oil*

10 Italian or Greek black olives, pitted and quartered

A generous handful of chopped fresh Italian parsley

*This would be ½ can of an Italian 150-gram canned tuna in olive oil. Use the other half for a sandwich or a salad. If you can find small cans, by all means stock them. The important thing is that the tuna be preserved in olive oil.

Bring a large pot of water with a tablespoon of salt to a boil. When it is boiling vigorously, drop in the pasta and stir it around.

Heat the oil in a medium skillet, and sauté the onion or shallot 3–4 minutes, until limp. Add the garlic slices and tomatoes and sauté another minute. Splash in the wine and cook down. Break up the tuna, and drop chunky flakes into the pan. Stir in the olives. Add at least ¼ cup of the pasta water to thin the sauce. When the pasta is done al dente (taste to be sure), transfer it with a big spider to the pan with the sauce, and stir it around, cooking the two together a minute. Add salt if needed, and more pasta water if the sauce is too dry. Spoon the pasta and sauce into a warm shallow bowl, and scatter parsley on top.

Fusilli with Mushrooms, Liver, and Cherry Tomatoes

WHAT YOU NEED

Salt	9 or 10 cherry tomatoes, halved
2 ounces fusilli or more, if wanted	1½–2 ounces leftover cooked
1 tablespoon olive oil	calf's liver, preferably pink in
6 medium cremini mushrooms,	the center
chopped	Freshly ground pepper
1 fat shallot, chopped	2–3 tablespoons grated
1 garlic clove, peeled and sliced	Parmesan
thin	

While the pasta is boiling in a large pot of salted water (see preceding recipe), heat the oil in a medium skillet, and sauté gently the mushrooms, shallot, and garlic, just until softened. Add the cherry tomatoes, and continue to sauté 3–4 minutes, until they have released their juice. Cut the liver into fairly small pieces, toss them into the pan, and season with salt and pepper. Remove from the heat, because you don't want the liver pieces to cook. When the pasta is done al dente, transfer it to the skillet with the sauce, and warm the two together, adding some pasta water if the sauce is too thin. Off heat, stir in half the cheese. Sprinkle on the rest just before eating.

Variation

If you don't have that leftover piece of calf's liver, use three or four chicken livers, in which case the livers need cooking. So, after the mushrooms, shallot, and garlic have softened, push them aside in the pan and brown the livers in the hot center of the pan, then break them up and finish cooking with the tomatoes.

Penne with Broccoli Rabe and Garlic

WHAT YOU NEED

Salt

6 branches broccoli rabe or
    broccolini

2–2½ ounces penne or other
    pasta

1 garlic clove, peeled and slivered

1 tablespoon olive oil

2 or 3 roasted garlic cloves*

Pinch of hot red-pepper flakes

¼ cup grated Parmesan, plus
    more as needed

*The roasted garlic is not essential to this dish, but I happened to have a freshly roasted head of garlic on hand one night when I was making this, and I felt it added a subtle, rich dimension.

Fill almost to the brim a large pot with salted water, and bring to a boil. Meanwhile, prepare the broccoli rabe by cutting off the stems and peeling them. When the water is boiling vigorously, put all the broccoli rabe in a strainer and set that into the boiling water. Blanch the broccoli for 1 minute, then remove and run cold water over it. This preliminary blanching sets the color and tames the bitterness, particularly in the broccoli rabe. After draining well, cut the branches and stems into 1-inch pieces. Now drop the penne in the boiling water, and while it is cooking, sauté the garlic slivers in the olive oil in a wok or a medium skillet. When the garlic is softened, add the broccoli rabe, and squeeze the roasted garlic out of its skin into the pan. Mix well, salt to taste, and scatter in the pepper flakes. Cook until the broccoli is just tender, then remove from the heat.

When the penne is done al dente, scoop it up and mix in with the greens. Heat through, then off heat, stir in about ¼ cup grated Parmesan. Remove to a warm pasta bowl, and sprinkle on more cheese if you like.

Linguine with Smoked Salmon Sauce

WHAT YOU NEED

Salt

2–3 ounces linguine

1 teaspoon butter

2 scallions, sliced fairly thin

A splash of vodka

2 or 3 slices smoked salmon

3–4 tablespoons heavy cream

Freshly ground pepper

1 teaspoon capers, rinsed

A scattering of chopped fresh
    parsley

While the linguine is boiling (see page 181), melt the butter in a small wok or a medium skillet. Toss in the scallions, and sauté gently for 1 minute, stirring. Splash in the vodka and let it cook down a little. Tear or cut the salmon into small bite-sized pieces, and stir them into the sauce. Pour in the cream and bring to a simmer. When the linguine is done al dente, scoop it up with a spider and tongs, letting the water drain

off, and mix it in with the sauce. Grind pepper generously over the pasta, and stir in the capers and parsley, then spoon it all up into a warm bowl.

Spaghettini with Cockles and Mussels, Alive, Alive O!

WHAT YOU NEED

2–3 ounces spaghettini

4 or 5 cockles (see variation)

¼ pound mussels

1 tablespoon olive oil

1 fat garlic clove, peeled and
  slivered

A generous splash of white wine

1 or 2 teaspoons butter

Freshly ground pepper

A handful of chopped fresh
  parsley

While the spaghettini is boiling (see page 181), rinse the cockles and mussels in a bowl of cold water, scrubbing away any grit and beard from the mussels. Heat the oil in a medium skillet or a small wok, and scatter in the garlic. Stir-fry for 1–2 minutes over medium heat, not letting the garlic brown. Splash in the wine and let it boil up, then dump in the cockles. Cover, and cook for 2 minutes before adding the mussels. Cook, covered, another few minutes, until the shells open (discard any that don't).

When the spaghettini is done al dente, scoop it up with a spider and tongs, and transfer it to the pan with the shellfish. Mix in 1 or 2 teaspoons butter. Let cook together a minute, spooning the juices over. Season with a few turns of the pepper grinder, and scatter parsley on top. Serve in a warm bowl.

Variation

Small clams can be used in place of the cockles, or make an all-clam or all-mussel sauce.

Barley

Barley is an ancient grain that has many uses in soups, casseroles, and salads, or as an accompaniment to meat. Today what we get is usually pearl barley, which has had the husk removed and therefore cooks more quickly. Its nutty flavor marries well with mushrooms, and I particularly like it with lamb.

Lamb, Mushroom, and Barley Casserole

Something to make when you have some leftover roast or shanks, this is a meal-in-one dish that can be eaten right from the individual small casserole dish it is baked in.

WHAT YOU NEED

½ cup barley

1½ cups lamb broth (see headnote, page 199) or leftover lamb gravy or pan juice with water

2 teaspoons butter or vegetable oil

1 shallot, or ½ small onion, chopped fine

3 or 4 mushrooms, quartered

A splash of white wine

½–¾ cup cooked lamb, cut into bite-sized pieces

Salt

Freshly ground pepper

A scattering of chopped fresh parsley mixed with a little savory or marjoram, fresh or dried

1 tablespoon breadcrumbs

A drizzle of olive oil

Simmer the barley in a small pot with most of the lamb broth, checking occasionally to see that the liquid has not boiled away, and adding more as needed. After 35–40 minutes, most of the liquid should be absorbed and the barley tender. Set aside. Meanwhile, heat the butter or oil in a small pan, and sauté the shallot until wilted. Add the mushrooms, and cook for 3–4 minutes, tossing occasionally. Splash in some white wine, and cook to reduce a little. Fill the bottom of a one-serving casserole with half the barley, then the mushrooms and lamb pieces, and finally the rest of the barley, seasoning each layer with salt and pepper and the herbs. Sprinkle the breadcrumbs on top, and drizzle a little olive oil over it. Bake in a preheated 350° oven for 20 minutes.

Couscous

Preparing a fine dish of Moroccan couscous used to be a labor of love—steaming, sifting, and fluffing up the little pearl granules made from semolina durum wheat all required quite a lot of time. But now we get a precooked couscous that takes minutes to prepare. It may not have quite the light finish of the old way, but it is a boon to a cook coming home at the end of a day and wanting to put an easy, well-balanced meal together. I remember Claudia Roden, years ago, introducing me to this North African grain product. We were cooking for a dinner party she was giving, working together in her comfortable kitchen, decorated with Middle Eastern tiles, at Wild Hatch, on the edge of Hampstead Heath in London. She had me fluffing the couscous, teaching me all the steps, as we gossiped and got to know each other better. It reminded me of her description—in her first, ground-breaking book, A Book of Middle Eastern Food*—of the women in her extended family in Cairo, where she grew up, who would spend afternoons shaping and stuffing tempting* mezze *pastries and enjoying every moment. I'm afraid we've forgotten how cooking together gives that kind of pleasure. But here's the easy formula for one serving of couscous.*

WHAT YOU NEED

Pinch of salt

⅔ cup couscous

1 teaspoon butter or olive oil

Heat ⅔ cup water and the salt in a small pot. As soon as it comes to a boil, sprinkle in the couscous and the butter or olive oil, and stir it around for ½ minute. Remove from the heat, cover, and let stand for 5 minutes. Fluff the couscous up with a fork, and it's all ready to go. It's good plain, or strewn with vegetables, and particularly delicious with stewed or braised leftover meats (see the recipe for Couscous with Lamb, Onions, and Raisins, page 52). It makes a nice salad, too, dressed with the same ingredients you might use for a Wild Rice Salad (page 179).

Farro

I had my first taste of farro, one of Lidia Bastianich's favorite grains, when we were doing photographs for her book *Lidia's Italy* and at lunch we sampled her superb dish of farro with cannellini beans, chickpeas, and mussels. I immediately tracked down some farro, and I have been playing with it since, coming up with some simple but wonderfully satisfying one-serving dishes that feature this barleylike grain, which tastes of the earth and of the sun.

Farro with Roasted Vegetables

WHAT YOU NEED

½ red bell pepper

1 large portobello mushroom, or
    2 or 3 shiitake mushrooms

1½ tablespoons olive oil

Salt

½ cup farro

½ bay leaf

Slice the red pepper in half lengthwise, and remove the stem and seeds. Cut off the mushroom stems (save for soup), and rub the pepper and mushrooms in a little of the olive oil and salt. Put the peppers on Silpat or parchment on a baking sheet, and roast in a preheated 425° oven. After 15 minutes, turn them, and place the mushrooms alongside, cap side up.

Meanwhile, rinse the farro, rubbing it through your fingers, and drain. Put it in a small pot with 1½ cups water, a good pinch of salt, the half-bay leaf, and the remaining olive oil, and bring to a boil. Lower the heat, and let simmer, covered, for 30 minutes, at which point the water should have boiled off (if not, pour it off) and the pepper and mushrooms should be roasted tender. Pull off the charred skin of the pepper slices. Spoon about half the farro into a soup bowl; arrange the mushrooms on top, along with the pepper pieces.

Variations

You can use other roasted vegetables to garnish the farro, or serve it plain as an accompaniment to meat.

Second Round

The portion of farro set aside makes a good salad with a small can of tuna fish scattered through it, along with a chopped ripe tomato, a scallion or two, and parsley. Toss gently with some vinaigrette dressing (page 149).

Polenta

Polenta—or cornmeal mush, to Southerners—is another great carrier for subtle flavors and leftover tidbits, as well as a soothing accompaniment to braised meats and poultry. But it's not for a weeknight dinner, because classic polenta requires long cooking with frequent stirring, and it's not easy to make a small amount. So I've found that a good solution is to make this baked polenta, or to use a quick-cooking polenta (see the recipe on page 195).

Baked Polenta with Vegetables

This recipe is inspired by one that Marion Cunningham created for her book Cooking with Children, *when she found that the youngsters in her cooking class didn't have the patience to stir and stir for 40 minutes. It makes a satisfying supper the first time around, and my version allows you to be flexible with the vegetable embellishments, so you use up some of your leftovers. If you want to have the treat of a delicious crispy polenta cake to enjoy later in the week, increase this recipe by adding an additional ¼ cup polenta and ¾ cup more warm water so you'll have that extra polenta to grill or fry.*

WHAT YOU NEED

1 ½ tablespoons olive oil

½ small onion, or 1 shallot, chopped

½ small tomato, chopped

3 tablespoons chopped cooked spinach, Swiss chard, or beet greens

3 or 4 strips roasted pepper chopped or other cooked

vegetables (see suggestions on page 194)

½ teaspoon salt, or more if needed

⅓ cup medium-grain polenta

1 cup warm water

2–3 tablespoons grated Parmesan cheese

Heat 1 tablespoon of the oil in a small skillet, and sauté the onion for a few minutes; then add the tomato and cook another 2 minutes. Mix in the additional cooked vegetables, salt lightly, and remove from the heat. Put the polenta in a smallish, rather shallow baking dish, and stir in the warm water and remaining olive oil. (Don't forget that if you want leftovers, add the additional amount of polenta and water.) Add the sautéed vegetables, sprinkle on the rest of the salt, and stir everything together. Bake in a preheated 350° oven for 25 minutes, then sprinkle Parmesan on top (I put the third tablespoon over the portion I am going to eat right away). Bake another 5 minutes, or until all the liquid has been absorbed. If I've made the larger amount of polenta, I scoop out the excess and put it aside, eating up all the vegetables with my polenta the first time around.

Variations

You can vary your cooked-vegetable additions to your heart's content—chopped asparagus spears or fiddleheads in spring, perhaps, quartered artichoke hearts, chunks of small zucchini, broccoli florets, and anything else the garden offers in summer. If you don't have roasted red pepper on hand, use about a quarter of a fresh bell pepper, any color, but sauté it first with the onion. If you want a more substantial dish, add some slivers of ham or slices of a cooked spicy sausage. Plan to eat all of these embellishments with your first serving, saving the pure polenta for later.

Second Round

BROILED OR FRIED POLENTA

Gather the remaining polenta in your hand, and gently shape it into an oval or round piece; if you have too much to handle in one piece, make two. Preheat your broiler. Brush the polenta lightly with olive oil, and set it on the broiler tray or on a baking sheet. Broil the polenta cake until browned and crusty on the top. If you want it doubly crisp, try turning it over and browning the other side. To fry it, film generously with oil a skillet large enough to hold the polenta. Heat the pan, and gently slip in the polenta cake. Fry until browned, then turn and do the other side. Serve with some juicy meat or poultry. Or try it with butter and warm maple syrup for breakfast.

A Quick Polenta Supper

Recently I've discovered an imported 1-minute polenta that works very well. So try it, and you can whip up a satisfying polenta supper in about 15 minutes.

WHAT YOU NEED

1 cup chicken broth

2 teaspoons light olive oil

1 small shallot

1 garlic clove, peeled and sliced
   thin

1 ripe plum tomato, chopped

About 1 cup shredded or
   chopped cooked meat, such as
   leftover braised lamb, beef, or
   veal, or poultry

A splash of red wine

⅓ cup 1-minute polenta

Pinch of salt

1 teaspoon butter

1 tablespoon grated Parmesan

Sprig of fresh basil, or a little
   chopped fresh parsley

Bring the broth to a simmer. Meanwhile, heat the oil in a small pan, and sauté the shallot for 1 minute, then add the garlic and the tomato, and sauté another 1–2 minutes (you want the tomato just barely cooked). Add the meat pieces and stir, then splash in the wine and cook down a little. By this time, the broth should be simmering. Pour in the polenta in a slow, steady stream as you stir constantly and continue to cook, stirring for a full minute. Remove the pan from the heat, add salt to taste, and stir in the butter and half the Parmesan. Spoon onto a warm plate, and arrange the meat garnish on top. Sprinkle on the remaining Parmesan, and top with a sprig of small basil leaves, if you have them; otherwise, use some chopped parsley.

Grits

I don't know any chef who travels with his own grits except Scott Peacock. And you can understand why. Once you have tasted those Southern stone-ground grits, it is hard to settle for less. But I hope he will forgive me for offering here a recipe for ordinary supermarket grits. They cook in 20 minutes, and I have borrowed Scott's method of cooking them partially in milk, which makes them so much creamier. This way, at least you may get so hooked on grits that you'll send away for the grittier stone-ground variety and give over part of a Sunday afternoon to stirring them as they cook slowly for a long time, the longer the better. Either way, grits are good with so many things—shrimp, chicken, game, pork, ham. I always make extra so that I can have some fried grits for breakfast the next day. Avoid instant grits and look for the old-fashioned ones.

WHAT YOU NEED

¾ cup milk	Salt
¾ cup water	1 or 2 tablespoons heavy cream
⅓ cup grits	A dollop of butter

Bring the milk and water to a boil in a 4-cup heavy pot. Lower the heat, and sprinkle the grits into the simmering liquid, stirring all the time until the liquid is absorbed. Cook slowly over low heat, stirring frequently, scraping the grits up from the bottom of the pan and adding a little water if they are sticking. After 20 minutes, they should be done. Salt to taste, stir in a tablespoon or more of the cream, and spoon up the portion you plan to eat right away, reserving the rest. Float a little butter on top.

Second Round

FRIED GRITS

First fry up two strips of bacon in a medium skillet. When it is evenly browned, remove the bacon to drain on a paper towel, leaving the fat in the pan. Scoop up the leftover grits, and form them into 2 hamburgerlike patties. Spread some flour on wax paper, season with a little salt and pepper, and dredge the grits cakes on both sides. Meanwhile, heat up the reserved bacon fat with about 2 teaspoons butter. When it is sizzling, lay in the grits cakes and cook until brown on both sides. Enjoy with warm maple syrup poured on top, and the bacon alongside.

Quinoa

Quinoa is a delightful grain from South America that hardly anyone here had heard of twenty years ago but which can now be found on most supermarket shelves. It can be used much as you would serve rice, but it has a lovely texture, and an almost nutty flavor that comes through when you toast the grains first. It is well worth that extra step, which takes only minutes.

Quinoa with a Lemony Flavor

¼ cup quinoa

½ cup boiling water

Pinch of salt

1 teaspoon small julienne of

lemon peel or of preserved-
lemon peel

1½ teaspoons fresh lemon juice

Pinch of saffron or turmeric

Heat a medium-small heavy skillet, and pour the quinoa into it. Let the grains heat slowly, swirling them around and back and forth until they start to pop and crackle and turn lightly brown. Remove from the heat, and transfer the toasted grains to a small heatproof baking dish with a tight-fitting lid. Pour the boiling water over, and stir in the salt, lemon peel, lemon juice, and saffron or turmeric. Cover (if the lid isn't tight, seal the top first with a piece of aluminum foil), and bake in a preheated 400° oven for 25 minutes.

I particularly like this surrounded by some roasted vegetables—a parsnip, a very small zucchini, a wide strip of red pepper, a slice of fennel. The vegetables, except for the zucchini, will take 5–10 minutes longer, so, after rubbing a little olive oil and salt over them, put them on a Silpat-lined baking sheet and start roasting them that much ahead, then slip the dish of quinoa alongside and let them finish roasting together.

BULGUR WHEAT

Bulgur wheat is cracked wheat that has been parboiled and parched, and then ground coarsely.

Bulgur Wheat with Leftover Lamb

Here's a dish I concocted when I had some leftover rare lamb from a roast. I had stripped most of the meat from the bone, but there was enough still clinging in the crevices to make a meaty broth, so I put the meat and the bone in a pot with an onion and a carrot, poured cold water over, and let it simmer for an hour or so. It made about 5 cups of lamb broth, most of which I stored in the freezer.

WHAT YOU NEED

1 tablespoon raisins

1 cup or more lamb broth or other meat stock thinned with water

½ cup bulgur wheat

1 tablespoon light olive oil

1 small onion

1 garlic clove, peeled and cut in thin slices

4 or 5 medium mushrooms, roughly chopped

4 or 5 chunks cooked lamb

½ teaspoon ground cinnamon

Salt and freshly ground pepper

A handful of young spinach leaves or watercress

1 tablespoon pine nuts

Soak the raisins in water to cover for 30 minutes. Meanwhile, bring ¾ cup of the lamb broth to a boil, and stir in the bulgur wheat. Cover, and cook at a lively simmer for 20 minutes, stirring now and then, and adding a little more broth if needed. While that's cooking, sauté the onion, garlic, and mushrooms in oil until softened. Add the lamb, and let brown a little, then sprinkle on the cinnamon, and salt and pepper to taste. Pour on

¼ cup broth. Drain the raisins, squeezing the water out, and add them. Simmer together a few minutes, then scatter the spinach leaves on top, cover, and cook just until the spinach has wilted, 1–2 minutes. Spoon into a warm bowl, and sprinkle pine nuts on top.

LEGUMES

The term *legume* refers to all plants that bear pods containing seeds or beans. They are cultivated all over the world, and some of the beans are eaten fresh, when in season, but mostly they are dried to be consumed throughout the year. Today we have a huge variety of legumes to choose from and lots of different ethnic cooking styles to draw on. Beans are a great convenience for the home cook looking for ways to create a new-tasting, nourishing dish out of yesterday's leftovers, and although the preliminary soaking and long cooking may seem a daunting task just for one, it's not the kind of preparation that requires careful tending. It's also nice to have extra cooked beans on hand for soups and salads and bean dishes such as the following.

Navy Beans with Duck-Leg Confit

This dish has much of the flavor of a cassoulet but is considerably simpler, because it uses ready-cooked duck-leg confit, which is obtainable today in most good markets and can also be ordered online.

WHAT YOU NEED

¼ cup dried navy, Great
 Northern, or cannellini
 beans
1 small onion, chopped
½ carrot, chopped
½ rib celery, chopped

2 garlic cloves, peeled and
 slivered
About ¾ cup duck or chicken
 stock
Salt and freshly ground pepper
1 duck-leg confit

Put the beans to soak overnight or during the workday in water to cover by several inches. Or use the "quick soak" method: put the beans in a pot with 2 cups water; bring to a boil, let boil for 2 minutes, then turn off the heat, cover, and let sit for 1 hour. When ready to cook, add the aromatic vegetables to the beans and their soaking water, plus about ½ cup of the stock, and cook at a lively simmer for almost 1 hour, or until just tender (taste to check), adding more stock as necessary. Season with salt and pepper. Set the duck-leg confit on top of the beans, cover, and simmer for about 10 minutes, until the duck is warmed through and has released its fatty flavor into the beans.

Second Round

If there is any left over, add it to a Winter Bean Soup (page 93).

Beans and Turkey Wings

This dish evolved when I had a good-sized holiday turkey left in the refrigerator. Somehow no one ever wants the wings. They're too big to gnaw on politely at the table, and the meat is hard to carve delicately into slices for sandwiches later. So they sit in the fridge, getting drier each day. But don't let that happen, because they make very good eating for one or two when they are properly reconstituted. And I found that well-flavored dried beans did the trick.

WHAT YOU NEED

½ cup dried beans, preferably smaller ones, such as navy beans or flageolets

1 medium onion, roughly chopped

2 garlic cloves, peeled and slivered

1 small carrot or ½ large carrot, peeled and chopped

Several fresh parsley stems

2 cooked turkey wings, trimmed (I use only the meaty sections)

Salt and freshly ground pepper

About 1 tablespoon leftover turkey gravy or broth, or 1 scant teaspoon *glace de viande* mixed with a little water

A sprinkling of chopped parsley leaves

Soak the beans in water to cover for 8–10 hours—overnight or during the workday, or use the quick-soak method in the preceding recipe, whatever is convenient. To cook, drain them and put them in a small heavy pot along with the onion, garlic, carrot, and parsley stems. Pour in enough water to cover by 1½ inches, and bring to a boil. Turn the heat down, and simmer, covered, for almost 1 hour, but taste after 50 minutes to see if they are tender. At this point, arrange the wings in a one-serving gratin dish, cover with foil, and set in a preheated 375° oven. Give them a 10-minute start to warm up, then cover them with the beans and their aromatic vegetables, seasoned with salt and pepper, and pour over them whatever small amount of bean juice you have left, fortified, if at all possible, with a little leftover gravy, or with one of the suggested substitutes. Make a loose cover of tented foil, and bake in the 375° oven for 20 minutes. Sprinkle some parsley on top.

Variations

You could use almost any kind of fowl, such as roast duck or goose wings, or some roast or braised meat. A few slices of cooked sausage are good, too.

Lentils

Unlike other legumes, lentils do not need to be soaked, so they are convenient when you are putting together a relatively quick meal.

WHAT YOU NEED

½ cup lentils, preferably French   Salt
2 cups water

Put the lentils in a small pot with the water, bring to a boil, and cook until tender, adding a little more water, if necessary. That could take anywhere from 25 to 35 minutes. If all the water hasn't been absorbed by the time the lentils are cooked, drain it off. Season the lentils with salt to taste.

Variations

WITH AN INDIAN ACCENT

For an Indian accent, add to a pot of ½ cup lentils and 1 cup water: ⅛ cinnamon stick, ¼ bay leaf, 1 peeled garlic clove, 1 thin slice peeled ginger, a pinch of turmeric, and salt and pepper. Top with a small sprinkling of toasted cumin. This is good with rice.

LAMB AND LENTILS
See page 47.

LENTIL SALAD WITH ROASTED GARLIC
I prefer using French lentils here, but any kind will do. You can use left-over cooked lentils, but if they are refrigerator-cold, heat them and let them absorb the flavors. I like to eat this salad slightly warm, or at least at room temperature.

WHAT YOU NEED

Cooked lentils (see page 203)   2 scallions, chopped
Salt   3 or 4 small chunks goat cheese
6 roasted garlic cloves (page 143)
3 or 4 sprigs fresh parsley,
   chopped

DRESSING

1 roasted garlic clove   2 teaspoons red-wine vinegar
¼ teaspoon salt   2 tablespoons olive oil

GARNISH

A few black olives

Put the cooked lentils into a bowl, and season with salt. Squeeze the roasted garlic into the lentils, mix well, and fold in the parsley, scallions, and goat cheese. For the dressing, mash the garlic, and mix it with the salt, vinegar, and olive oil. Pour the dressing over the warm salad, using as much as you like. Garnish with a few black olives.

In my Vermont kitchen

Six Treats, Sweets, and Special Indulgences

Preserved Lemons

Roasted Red Peppers

Soft-Shell Crabs

EXPERIMENTING WITH A JAPANESE FISH

Sautéed Scallops

Shad Roe with Sorrel Sauce

SEA URCHINS

Osso Buco with Gremolata

A Small Cassoulet

Braised Sweetbreads Marsala with Honey Mushrooms

Steamed Lobster

This final chapter is a catchall of things I might make on a lazy Sunday, or whenever I have time to give myself over to cooking. I love making bread, to feel it come together as I knead it rhythmically and shape it into small baguettes, first tearing off a hunk to make myself a small pizza for lunch. Sunday's a day when I might have a special breakfast of popovers, or blueberry muffins, or crêpes with maple syrup. And it's also a time to make some cookies, not just for myself but for anyone who may drop by hungry.

On weekends, I try to check out my larder, and if something is running low, such as tomato sauce or white sauce/béchamel or chicken broth, I plan meals that call for some of these essentials so I can make extra to replenish my stock.

Usually I end my dinner with some good cheese and fruit. But occasionally I have a yen for something sweet, particularly a homemade dessert that arouses such strong taste memories that as soon as you take your first bite you are mysteriously transported. So I have gathered here a few of those treasured desserts that do well reduced to a single helping or two. I hope that you'll try them, and that they will encourage you to experiment with some of the desserts from your own past that you would particularly like to re-create for one.

Finally, there are certain foods that we all crave yet tend to steer away from because they seem so extravagant. Remember, though, that you're feeding only one, and a fresh lobster is not too much of an extravagance. So be good to yourself, and enjoy that lobster—and other special indulgences.

French Breads and Pizzas

What could be more appealing on a weekend than to fill the kitchen with the good smell of bread baking? I like to start my bread dough when I get up, and for lunch I reward myself with a fresh-from-the-oven pizza. Perhaps I'll share a baguette over dinner with friends, and have some mini-loaves to put in the freezer and enjoy in the weeks ahead—all made from the same dough. If there are children around, I announce what I'm up to, and invariably they will want to join me and pitch in. For them, there is something magical about making bread—the way it rises quietly in a bowl under a cover, the fun of punching the dough down, forming the loaves, and creating steam in the oven just before baking. To say nothing of how good it tastes.

I started baking bread in the sixties, when I persuaded Julia Child to work out a recipe for French bread that could be baked in an American home oven. In those days, it was almost impossible to buy a crusty baguette. Now there are artisan bakers all over who have mastered the techniques, and there's really no need to bake one's own. But it is such fun.

WHAT YOU NEED

1 package (1 scant tablespoon) active dry yeast
1¼ cups warm water
2 teaspoons kosher salt

3 tablespoons whole-wheat flour
3–3½ cups all-purpose white flour

Put the yeast and ¼ cup of the warm water in a large bowl (or the bowl of an electric mixer, if you want to use that), and stir it around with your finger to make sure it dissolves. Add the remaining water, the salt, the whole-wheat flour, and 3 cups of the white flour. Mix well, adding more white flour if the dough seems too wet. It should be a moist dough that you can handle with floured hands. Now knead it by hand, on a floured work surface, or in the mixer, using the dough hook (you can also use a large food processor). Continue to knead until the dough is smooth and elastic, 8–10 minutes, flouring as necessary but still keeping the dough moist; use a light touch.

Clean your mixing bowl, and return the dough to it. Cover the bowl with a kitchen towel or plastic wrap, and let the dough rise at room temperature, or even a bit cooler than that if possible, until tripled in size. At this point, if you want a pizza, cut off a piece (or two) of dough a little smaller than a baseball, and follow the directions on the facing page for making it. Return the bulk of the dough to the clean bowl, cover, and let rise again, this time until doubled in volume.

After the second rise, turn the dough out and punch it down. If you have extracted dough for two small pizzas or one larger one, you'll have enough left for four mini-baguettes and one 15-inch baguette.

For the minis, tear off four pieces of dough smaller than a baseball. Pat them into flat ovals, fold in half lengthwise, and pinch the ends and seam to hold the dough together. With your hands, roll each one out into a small baguette shape about 4 inches long. Arrange the loaves, pinched side down, on a floured kitchen towel, leaving space between, and drape another towel on top. Let rise for 30 minutes.

To make the 15-inch baguette, pat the dough into an oval, fold in half lengthwise, and pinch the ends together. Now make a lengthwise trench with the side of your hand down the middle, again fold lengthwise over the trench, and pinch the ends together. Flour your work surface again, and roll the dough out with your floured hands, starting in the center and moving them outward as you roll to a length of about 15 inches. Transfer the dough to a floured kitchen towel, positioning it seam side up, and fold the towel over to cover. Let rise for 30 minutes. Meanwhile, if you have a large baking stone, slide it onto your oven rack and preheat the oven to 450°. If you don't have a stone, use a baking sheet and let it preheat.

When you are ready to bake, sprinkle cornmeal along the far long side of another baking sheet, and with the help of the kitchen towel, flip the bigger baguette over onto it. Make three diagonal slashes across the top of the dough, then, holding the pan over the hot baking stone or sheet, jerk it so that the baguette slips off and onto the hot surface. Shut the oven door quickly while you transfer the mini-baguettes to the baking stone in the same way, slashing each of them just once across the top diagonally.

Now you have to create some steam. The simplest way is to put about a dozen ice cubes into a roasting pan and set that on the oven floor. I have an old-fashioned iron (pre-electric) that I heat up on one of the rings of my gas stove full-force for at least 15 minutes, and when all the baguettes are in the oven, I slip in a pan of cold water and with tongs pick up my fiercely hot iron and plop it into the pan. A great whoosh of steam rises, and I shut the door quickly.

Remove the small breads after 15 minutes, and let the full-sized baguette bake another 10 minutes. Cool all the loaves on a cooling rack.

TO MAKE PIZZAS

Either make two small pizzas or one larger one with the dough you have set aside. Pat, roll, and, if you feel daring, twirl on your fist the piece of dough for a pizza until you have shaped it into a fairly thin circle of dough the size you want—about 5 inches for the smaller pizza. Set it on a baking sheet or in a tart pan with a removable rim or on a paddle sprinkled with cornmeal, and lightly brush a little olive oil over the surface. Now fill it with whatever you have on hand that appeals to you: a small fresh tomato, sliced, or a couple of spoonfuls of tomato sauce; cheeses that need to be consumed (you'll be surprised at how many cheeses are good on pizza— and you can use more than one); if you want meat, strips of ham, prosciutto, and sausage are all good; lightly cooked aromatic vegetables such as artichoke hearts, leeks, mushrooms of all kinds, and tangy greens marry well with other filling elements, or are good just alone; and eggplant, along with strips of roasted peppers or some ratatouille (page 132), is the best. Don't forget possibly using condiments such as black or green olives as an accent. When you've filled up that circle of dough, put the baking sheet or the tart pan bottom (remove the rim) in the oven. Or, if the pizza is on a paddle and you are using a baking stone, slip the pizza onto

the hot stone, using a firm jerking motion (and maybe the help of a spatula to get it there with the topping intact). Bake at the hottest setting of your oven (preheated) for about 12 minutes or until the dough around the edge is crusty and lightly browned. Remove with tongs or a spatula and eat warm.

Seeded Bread

When I have the urge to bake bread on a weekend and want something not quite so time-consuming as French bread, I often make this loaf. It is a healthy bread with a good texture and makes particularly delicious sandwiches. It is also great toasted for breakfast.

WHAT YOU NEED

1 tablespoon active dry yeast	3 cups whole-wheat flour
3 cups warm water	2–3 cups all-purpose white flour
3 tablespoons soft butter or vegetable oil, plus a little for the mixing bowl and pans	1/3 cup wheat germ
	1/2 cup sunflower seeds
	1/4 cup sesame seeds
1/4 cup dark maple syrup, molasses, or honey	1/4 cup flax seeds or poppy seeds
	1 teaspoon salt

Makes two 8-inch loaves

Pour the yeast into the bowl of a standing electric mixer, if you're using one, or otherwise just put it in a big bowl. Pour 1/4 cup of the warm water over the yeast, and let sit until dissolved and bubbly.

Add the rest of the water, the butter or oil, the syrup, all the whole-wheat flour, and 2 cups of the white flour, as well as the wheat germ, the seeds, and the salt. Mix well, and knead in the mixer or turn out and knead by hand, adding as much of the remaining white flour as the dough wants to absorb. Even if you knead in the mixer, turn out the dough at the end and knead it it briefly by hand, to get the feel of it. This will be a dense, heavy dough, but don't worry—it will rise. Butter or oil the mixing bowl, and return the dough to it. Cover with plastic wrap, and let rise at room temperature until doubled in volume.

Punch down and divide the dough in half. Butter thoroughly two 8- or 9-inch bread pans. Shape each piece into a loaf: first pat it into an oval the length of your bread pan, then with your hands stretch and ease the long sides under and pinch the seams together on the bottom side. Place each loaf in a bread pan seamside down.

Cover the pans loosely with a kitchen towel, and let rise again until the dough has begun to swell over the top of the pans. Bake in a preheated 350° oven for 45 minutes. Turn the loaves out onto a rack to cool before slicing.

OPTIONS

A loaf of this bread, tightly wrapped in plastic wrap, will keep through the week stored in the refrigerator. I usually freeze the second loaf, cutting it in half or in thirds first and wrapping each separately. Or I give the second loaf to a bread-loving friend.

Popovers

All of us yearn sometimes for a particular remembered taste, and we want to re-create it. I feel that way about popovers, perhaps because they are associated with memories of family discussions about the way to obtain the perfect popover (they all tasted good to me). My aunt Lucy in Barre, Vermont, was thrilled when she got a new state-of-the-art stove and discovered that her popovers could go into a cold oven the night before. All she had to do was set the time and then press a button so that the oven would turn on magically and have the popovers baked in time for breakfast. But my aunt Marian, seven miles away in Montpelier, insisted that you couldn't put popovers into a cold oven. And they had a competition that, as I remember, didn't prove anything one way or the other. In more recent years, Marion Cunningham discovered that the secret to a high rise and a crispy exterior was to use Pyrex cups set at a distance from one another, so the heat could circulate. Naturally, a new popover pan was soon on the market based on that principle. Even more significant, at least for the single cook, was her discovery that if you prick the popovers in several places with a knife as soon as they emerge from the oven, the steam will escape and the popovers will not turn soggy—a valuable tip if you want to reheat one to enjoy the next day. But they don't keep long, so when I'm alone I make just two in my new popover-pan cups and have one piping hot for dinner (it's particularly good with red meat, reminding me of our family Sunday dinners of roast beef and Yorkshire pudding) and heat up the other the next morning for breakfast, to be eaten with soft butter and my own gooseberry jam. Who could ask for anything more?

WHAT YOU NEED

1 large egg

⅓ cup milk

Good pinch of salt

⅓ cup all-purpose flour

Soft butter

Preheat the oven to 400° (I'm using the old-fashioned Aunt Marian method). Beat the egg thoroughly, then add the milk and blend. Stir in the salt and flour and mix until smooth. Butter either two Pyrex cups (2 inches high, top diameter 3½ inches) or two of the cups in a popover pan, and pour equal amounts of batter into each. Set the cups on a baking sheet in the middle rack of the oven, or just slip the popover pan onto the middle rack. Bake for 25 minutes. The popovers should be almost tripled in height and lightly browned. Remove from the oven, turn out the popovers, and prick them with the point of a knife in several places. If you are putting one away for the next day, wrap it loosely in paper—not plastic—and leave it at room temperature.

Putting Yesterday's Bread to Work

Buying bread can be a problem for the single cook, because seldom does one encounter small loaves. But even though there's nothing like a fresh loaf, bread does freeze well. What I usually do is buy a baguette or some other crusty loaf, and what I don't eat the first day I'll cut into four or five pieces, wrap the pieces separately tightly in foil, then put the pieces in a freezer bag and freeze. That way, I can pull one out in the morning so it's ready for supper, heated up a touch. I'll do the same with a loaf of sandwich bread, although that keeps longer, so I'll probably freeze it in half-loaves. If I feel I need the comfort of making my own French bread, I'll do so and form the dough into small one-portion baguettes for the freezer (see page 209).

Of course, there are lots of uses for slightly stale bread:

- Make breadcrumbs. Just remove the crusts, break up the bread, and spin it in a blender or a food processor until reduced to crumbs. You can keep small packets of breadcrumbs in the freezer.
- Use chunks of day-old bread in a salad or in a soup. For a salad, let the bread soak in the dressing, enough to saturate and soften.
- Make croutons: Slice the bread, rub some olive oil on top, and perhaps some garlic mashed with salt, and toast in the oven. Great for soups, particularly with *pistou* slathered on top for a bouillabaisse (see page 91).
- Use toasted slices as a base for minced meats, mushrooms, or other slightly saucy delights.
- Make a stuffing for some poultry, meat, fish, or a vegetable.
- Make a bread-and-butter pudding, Apple Maple Bread Pudding (page 233), or a Summer Pudding (page 234).

Your bread will never go to waste!

Berry Muffins

I usually make these in the summer, when berries are plentiful and bursting with flavor. I gather the berries and put all the ingredients out the night before, and it takes but a few minutes to whip up the batter. Then there's time to go for a swim and work up an appetite while the muffins bake. If you have family and guests around, just double the recipe. This more modest amount will give you a dozen mini-muffins, which I prefer, plus two regular-sized ones that I bake in small Pyrex cups. If you don't eat them all, they freeze well.

WHAT YOU NEED

1 cup flour

1 ½ teaspoons baking powder

Good pinch of salt

1 large egg

½ cup milk or cream, or part milk and cream

2 ½ tablespoons sugar

2 tablespoons melted butter, plus soft butter for greasing the muffin tins

½ teaspoon vanilla extract

¾ cup blueberries, raspberries, blackberries, or gooseberries

Topping: 4 or 5 crushed sugar cubes, preferably cubes that have been stored with a vanilla bean (see page 224)

Toss the flour, baking powder, and salt together. Break the egg into a bowl, and beat in the milk, sugar, melted butter, and vanilla. Don't over-mix; a few lumps are welcome. Fold in the berries. (If you are using gooseberries, crush them slightly first, and roll them in at least 2 tablespoons more sugar, because they are very tart.) Butter a twelve-cup mini-muffin pan plus two Pyrex cups—or, if you prefer, eight cups of a standard muffin pan—and spoon in the batter. The mini-cups can be filled to the top; the regular cups should be three-quarters full. Bake in a preheated 400° oven. The minis should be done in 20 minutes; the regulars, 25 minutes. Sprinkle the crushed sugar on top. Eat warm with sweet butter.

Ways of Using Up Milk

Milk is an essential component in so many recipes that you feel obliged to have it on hand, even if you're not a steady milk drinker. Most supermarkets no longer carry half-pint or even pint sizes, so we are coerced into buying at least a full quart and then see most of it go to waste. But there are ways to use up that milk before it turns sour. Here are some of my strategies:

MAKING YOGURT

I eat a lot of yogurt, so making my own is a good way for me to use up the extra milk. And it is so easy. You just have to save a tablespoon of any whole-milk, nonsweetened yogurt you have, and use that as a starter to convert 3 cups of milk into a bowl of silky yogurt. Heat the milk just to the boiling point, and when bubbles appear around the edge, remove it from the heat. Pour the milk into a bowl, and let stand at room temperature until it is cool enough for you to plunge your finger in and hold it there comfortably. If you feel more secure using a thermometer, do so; the temperature should be about 105°. At this point, extract ½ cup of the warm milk, and whisk it in a small bowl with the tablespoonful of yogurt. Now return the milk-and-yogurt mix to the bowl of warm milk, and blend thoroughly with your whisk. Cover the bowl with plastic wrap, and leave undisturbed in a warm place for 6–8 hours. I put mine in a turned-off oven that has a pilot light, and this is perfect. If you have not got a similar warm spot, cover the bowl with a blanket, and keep it in your warmest room, with the radiator going. After 6 hours, the yogurt should have set. If you want to leave it longer, it will develop a slightly more sour taste. You can, of course, make two or three times the amount I describe here. I chose 3 cups because that's about the amount I usually have left in my milk carton. You can also let the yogurt set in individual cups instead of a bowl. And you can pour off some of the excess whey if you like your yogurt more firm.

Try to use *whole*-milk yogurt as your starter; if you are on a strict regimen, you can use low-fat milk. But don't let your supermarket dictate to you. I remember how furious the imposing James Beard was when he could find only the low-fat stuff in the supermarket case. The manager was summoned, and Jim stared down on him, shaking his finger, and said: "Look here, you're not my doctor."

MAKING CREAM SAUCE

Before that milk turns, you might want to make cream sauce, both for immediate use plus to stash some away in the freezer (see page 164).

MAKING A SPECIAL NOSTALGIC DESSERT

Bread pudding or, better, an Apple Maple Bread Pudding (page 233), sounds tempting to me, and it will help you to eat up some leftover bread, too. It's best made in two portions. Share it with a friend, or eat one still warm from the oven and have the second one cold later in the week.

Icebox Cookies

The correct term for these cookies today is, of course, "refrigerator cookies," but I cling to "icebox" because it reminds me of the old ice chest that we used during summers in Vermont. The dough is wrapped in wax paper and chilled. Then you slice the cookies as thin as you like, and as many as you want. Bake only what you figure you will eat in the next few days and then cut and bake another batch, so the cookies are always fresh—a boon to the single cook. You can play with the dough, too, and vary the ingredients, so you never tire of exactly the same flavor. Here is an almondy-tasting version that I particularly like.

WHAT YOU NEED

¼ pound butter, at room temperature

⅓ cup dark-brown sugar

⅓ cup granulated sugar

1 teaspoon almond extract

1 large egg

¼ teaspoon cream of tartar

¼ teaspoon salt

¼ teaspoon freshly grated nutmeg

1½ cups all-purpose flour

½ cup slivered almonds

Cream the butter and the two sugars together in a bowl. Add the almond extract, crack the egg into the bowl, and mix thoroughly. Toss the cream of tartar, salt, and nutmeg with the flour, add to the batter and beat until blended. Fold in the slivered almonds. Turn the dough out onto a large piece of lightly floured wax paper, and with floured hands form it into a long roll about 1½ inches in diameter (or, if you prefer, form two rolls). Now wrap the wax paper around the log, and refrigerate for several hours or for as many as 10 days (then if not used up, it should be frozen).

When you are ready to bake a batch, preheat the oven to 400°. Using a sharp knife, cut as many ¼-inch slices of the dough to make as many cookies as you think you'll eat up in the next few days, and arrange the rounds with space between on a cookie sheet lined with Silpat or parchment. Bake for 8 minutes. Remove to a rack to cool.

Variations

To vary, look through some old American cookbooks—*Fannie Farmer,* the original *Joy of Cooking*—for ideas. I love the oatmeal combination recommended in *Joy,* and I've made the spicy version using dark Vermont maple syrup instead of molasses. There are lots of possibilities.

Biscotti

I find today that of all cookies, Italian biscotti are the most tempting to make, because they keep so well. "Biscotti" means "twice cooked," and what makes them so absorbent, to say nothing of imperishable, is that they are baked twice. Moreover, the true biscotti have no fat in them (although American versions tend to sneak some in), and that is why they hold their own when dunked into a cup of afternoon tea or after-dinner coffee. So here is the real thing, to savor for the weeks ahead.

WHAT YOU NEED

2¼–2½ cups all-purpose flour	3 large eggs
1 cup sugar	1 teaspoon vanilla extract
2 teaspoons cream of tartar	1 orange
1 teaspoon baking soda	1½ cups toasted hazelnuts
½ teaspoon salt	and/or walnuts

Put 2¼ cups of the flour with the sugar, cream of tartar, baking soda, and salt into a mixing bowl or the bowl of an electric mixer, and blend well. Whisk the eggs in a separate bowl, just enough to blend yolks and whites, and then set aside 1 tablespoon for the final glazing. Pour the remaining eggs and the vanilla into the dry ingredients, and mix until the dough comes together. If it seems too wet to pick up and knead, add a little more flour; if it seems too dry, sprinkle a little water onto the dry spots. Knead a few turns with floured hands. Now grate the peel of the orange (I use the coarse holes of a box grater, because I like larger pieces of orange than fine grating gives). Chop the nuts into coarse pieces, and knead them into the dough along with the grated orange to distribute evenly. Divide the dough in half, and form two logs approximately 10 inches long. Put them on a parchment- or Silpat-lined baking sheet, several inches apart, and paint the sides and tops with the reserved egg glaze. Bake in a preheated 350° oven for 30 minutes. Turn the oven down to 300°, and remove the two pieces to cool on a rack for 10 minutes. When they have cooled, use a serrated bread knife to cut diagonal slices a little more than ½ inch thick, and lay them out flat on a large cookie sheet. Return them to the oven for 15 minutes. Remove, and cool on a rack thoroughly before storing in a large cookie tin.

Variations

You can use different nuts and raisins in the dough, as well as grated lemon, or make chocolate dough, adding ¼ cup melted chocolate chips to the dough and working in some broken-up chocolate.

Peanut Butter Cookies

Recently, when I came upon a jar of peanut butter that had been around awhile, my New England frugality wouldn't let me throw it out; instead visions of peanut butter cookies danced in my head. I hadn't made them in years, and I discovered they are well worth reviving.

WHAT YOU NEED

8 tablespoons butter, at room temperature

½ cup granulated sugar

½ cup dark-brown sugar

1 large egg

½ cup peanut butter

1½ cups all-purpose flour

Pinch of salt

1 teaspoon baking powder

About 12 sugar cubes (preferably vanilla sugar, page 224), crushed with a rolling pin

Put the butter in the bowl of an electric mixer, and cream it. Add the two sugars, and continue to beat until well mixed. Crack the egg into the bowl, add the peanut butter, and beat until smooth. Toss the flour, salt, and baking powder together on a piece of wax paper, then pick it up and form a spout so you can pour the dry ingredients alternately with the egg–peanut butter mixture into the mixer bowl as it is going. Mix until blended.

With your hands or with a small scoop, pick up equal-sized pieces of the cookie batter smaller than a golf ball. Roll them a few at a time in the crumbled sugar cubes and arrange them on buttered or Silpat-lined baking sheets, 2 inches between cookies. Repeat until you have used up all the batter. Now, with the tines of a fork laid flat on top of each cookie, make a crisscross pattern, first going one way, then the other. You may need to flour the fork if your dough gets sticky. Bake in a preheated 375° oven for 10 minutes, until just lightly browned; you may want to give them another minute, switching the pans around. Let cool on a cookie rack and store in a cookie jar.

Vanilla Sugar

Edna Lewis taught me the useful trick of keeping sugar cubes with a whole vanilla bean or two in a tight jar. Then, when you want a sugar coating to top a pudding, muffins, or cookies, you just extract the cubes you need, whack them with a large rolling pin, and roll them out to whatever consistency you want. This gives the sugar coating a real crunch and a jolt of vanilla flavor. Replenish the bean in the jar when it gets tired, but it'll give flavor for a long time.

Some Practical Tips to Save on Cleanup

One of the complaints I hear about home cooking is that it's so messy and time-consuming, particularly all that washing up. And just for one? Most recipes call for more bowls than you may have on your shelf. I find that if you line things up on a work surface close to your stove, you don't need all those bowls. And in making recipes for breads, pastries, and the like, wax paper comes in very handy. You can toss the dry ingredients together on a large piece of wax paper, then pick it up carefully, and funnel the dry ingredients into the bowl of your mixer while it is running.

You'll notice that I often call for Silpat mats to line a baking sheet. I keep one mat for roasting or broiling savory foods, and a couple more for baking cookies and pastries. They are very easy to rinse off and last a long time. You can use parchment or greased aluminum foil instead.

Schrafft's Oatmeal, Raisin, and Walnut Cookies

I find that most store-bought oatmeal cookies can't touch the rich homemade variety I remember from my childhood. We used to get them at the old Schrafft's stores, and when I asked Jim Beard if he remembered those cookies and, if so, could he give me the recipe, he immediately called the head of the company and got a formula for producing a huge amount. Jim helped translate some of the unfamiliar ingredients and reduce the recipe to a manageable amount. I have been making this oatmeal cookie ever since—now in small amounts. Double the recipe if you have children around.

WHAT YOU NEED

4 tablespoons butter (½ stick)

½ cup sugar

1 large egg

½ teaspoon vanilla extract

2 tablespoons milk

¾ cup oatmeal (not instant-cooking)

¾ cup all-purpose flour

¼ teaspoon baking powder

¼ teaspoon baking soda

½ teaspoon salt

½ teaspoon ground cinnamon

¼ teaspoon ground allspice

½ cup raisins

½ cup chopped walnuts

Beat the butter and sugar together in a mixing bowl. Add the egg, vanilla, and milk, and beat until light and fluffy. Stir in the oatmeal. Mix the flour, baking powder and soda, salt, and spices on a piece of wax paper, then pick that up and dump the dry ingredients into your mixing bowl. Beat until well blended. Fold in the raisins and walnuts.

Drop the cookie batter by the tablespoonful onto Silpat-lined baking sheets (or just butter the baking sheets), leaving about 1½ inches between mounds. Bake in a preheated 350° oven for 12 minutes. Remove the cookies, and cool on racks.

Pastry Dough

I make this pastry dough on a leisurely weekend when I want to treat myself to a small quiche for lunch, or a fruit pastry for dessert. Then I store the rest of the dough in the freezer, so I'll have it on hand if family or friends show up unexpectedly, or if I feel like making something for myself one night that requires a pastry topping, such as Beef and Kidney Pie (page 34). I use a food processor to make the dough, because it is so easy, and if you measure the pulses carefully as you are mixing the dough, you can't go wrong. I learned from Lydie Marshall, that incomparable French-cooking teacher, the trick of saying "alligator" out loud to determine the length of each pulse.

WHAT YOU NEED

2 cups all-purpose flour

½ teaspoon salt

14 tablespoons (1¾ sticks) very cold unsalted butter

3 or 4 tablespoons cold water

Spin the flour and salt in the food processor for a few seconds to mix. Cut the butter, which should be very cold, lengthwise in quarters, then cut it quickly into small chunks and dump them in with the flour. Process in spurts eight times, pulsing just long enough to say "alligator." Put an ice cube in a cup with 3 tablespoons water, then sprinkle the water over the dough. Pulse again 8 times, saying "alligator" each time. Turn the dough out onto a lightly floured work surface, and gather it together. If you find that there are dry spots where the dough won't hold together, sprinkle up to 1 tablespoon more ice water over the dry areas.

Now you are going to perform what the French call the *fraisage,* meaning that you smear the dough out in fairly small increments, then gather it together again. When it has all been smeared, cut off the amount of dough you will be using for your immediate need, shape it into a flat disk, wrap it in wax paper, and refrigerate for 30 minutes before rolling it out. Freeze the remaining dough in however many pieces you wish, wrapping each disk tightly in plastic wrap.

Quiche for One

Quiche for one? That sounds ambitious, but the truth is, it's a cinch to make yourself a small quiche if you have an individual tart pan, about 4 inches in diameter, with a removable bottom, and some excess tart dough in your freezer. And what a treat it is.

WHAT YOU NEED

About 2 ounces Pastry Dough
   (preceding recipe); if frozen,
   take out in the morning and
   defrost slowly in the fridge
1 large egg
¼–⅓ cup heavy cream
¼ teaspoon salt

A sprinkling of freshly grated
   nutmeg
About 1½ slices prosciutto
   or ham, torn in small bits,
   or 2 slices bacon, cooked and
   crumbled

Preheat the oven to 450°. If the dough is very cold, let it warm up in the kitchen until it feels pliable. Roll it out on a lightly floured board to a circle approximately 9 inches in diameter, and fit it into the small tart form, pressing it firmly around the edges, trimming the overhang. Prick the bottom, then line the pan with foil buttered on its underside and fill it with dried beans or small baking stones. Bake for 10 minutes at 425°, turn down the heat to 375°, remove the foil and beans, prick the bottom again, and bake another 2 minutes.

Meanwhile, as the shell is baking, crack the egg into a measuring cup, and add enough cream to make a scant ½ cup. Add the seasonings, and mix well. Scatter the prosciutto, ham, or bacon over the bottom of the tart, and pour in the egg-cream mixture, which will fill the tart shell right up to the top (if you have a little too much, just discard or add it to some scrambled eggs). Place on a Silpat- or foil-lined baking pan and bake for 25 minutes. Remove from the oven and let set for about 5 minutes, if you can wait that long before you dive in.

Variations

A quiche is a great catchall for goodies lurking in the fridge. You can vary the above just by adding a tablespoon or so of grated cheese—Gruyère, aged Cheddar or Gouda, or a French mountain cheese—you name it. Sautéed mushrooms, cooked asparagus, spinach, and zucchini make good fillings, as do cooked seafood, sausage, and spicy meats.

Individual Apple Tart

I can't resist making this special tart for myself when my Duchess apple tree in Vermont is laden with the most flavorful apples I've ever tasted. I've never sprayed the tree, so, yes, there are what we call wormholes, but I peel around them or dig out the dark tunnels with the point of a knife.

If you're using a frozen portion of your own tart dough, remember to take it out in the morning and let it defrost at room temperature. If you're making up a new batch, be sure to make extra to put away for a repeat performance.

WHAT YOU NEED

2½–3 ounces Pastry Dough
  (page 226)
1 heaping tablespoon tart jam or
  jelly (I use my own Gooseberry
  Jam, page 240)

1 tart apple
About 2 teaspoons sugar

Roll the pastry out into a circle, about 6½ inches in diameter, and place it on a baking sheet. To measure the circle precisely and trim it, put a plate, approximately 6 inches in diameter, on top, and then cut with a sharp knife all around the circumference and remove excess dough to make a neat circle. Dip a pastry brush into the jam or jelly, and paint the bottom of the dough, leaving a ¼-inch edge unpainted all around. Quarter the apple, peel and core it, and cut it into fairly thin slices. Arrange the slices overlapping in a circle all around the pastry round, leaving the ¼-inch border, and then arrange the remaining slices in the center of the dough. Sprinkle up to 2 teaspoons of sugar on top, using more or less according to how tart your apples are. Place on a baking sheet, and bake in a pre-heated 425° oven for 10 minutes, then lower the heat to 375° and bake 20 more minutes. Eat it while warm.

Variations

Individual fruit tarts can be made the same way with rhubarb and pears. I prefer to use berries such as strawberries and raspberries raw in a tart, so I simply pre-bake the painted circle of dough, pricking the bottom first, for about 20 minutes at 425°, then, when the crust is cool, I arrange the berries on top. Gooseberries, however, are best cooked in the tart and need three times the amount of sugar.

Crêpes

I prefer thin French pancakes to the more doughy American kind, so I often make a batch of crêpe batter for a Sunday breakfast and have plenty left over to whip up a rolled savory crêpe filled with some leftover that needs dressing up, or a sweet version enrobing some fruit or berries. For breakfast, I slather a warm crêpe with yogurt—preferably Greek-style, because it's less runny—put another crêpe on top and more yogurt, and leave the final layer bare to catch the warm maple syrup I pour over it. A few berries scattered around complete the picture.

I remember how James Beard would teach the making and baking of crêpes and pancakes in his opening class for beginners. He liked the students to observe what happened when the batter—some with baking powder, as in American pancakes; some not, as in French crêpes—hit the hot surface of the pan and baked: one rising perceptibly, the other hardly at all but acquiring a crisper tan. And he would prowl around among the students, encouraging them to use their fingers to turn the crêpe and get the feel of the texture. The "nervous Nellies," as Julia Child always called them, held back, but the intrepid relished the quick finger-flip, and you could tell that they were the ones who were really going to enjoy cooking.

FOR THE BATTER

⅔ cup all-purpose flour	1 tablespoon melted butter
⅓ cup milk	Pinch of salt
⅓ cup water	For frying: a little butter or
1 egg	vegetable oil

Put all the ingredients for the batter into a blender, and blend for at least 1 minute or use a food processor or beat by hand. Let rest in the fridge several hours before using, or refrigerate overnight. Heat a 6- or 8-inch skillet, depending on what size pancakes you want, preferably nonstick, and brush a little butter or oil over the bottom. When the pan is hot but not smoking, pour just enough batter into it to cover the bottom, tipping the pan and swirling the batter around to distribute it evenly in a thin layer. Cook over medium-high heat until bubbles appear on the surface and the bottom is lightly browned, then flip the crêpe over onto the other side. You can do this by jerking the pan, but it takes practice, so don't hesitate to use a spatula—or your fingers. When the bottom side is lightly browned, remove the crêpe to a warm plate, and continue to make as many more as you wish, stacking them as they are done.

Pear Crisp

Crisps and crumbles—they are one and the same—were always a favorite in our family, and I miss having them on a regular basis. But I found it's very easy to make just one portion in a small casserole dish (I use an onion-soup bowl).

WHAT YOU NEED

1 just-ripened, firm pear	1 tablespoon water
2 teaspoons sugar	Freshly grated nutmeg

TOPPING	GARNISH
1 tablespoon butter	Heavy cream
3 tablespoons flour	
3½ tablespoons sugar	

Peel the pear, core it, remove the seeds, and cut it into rough pieces. Toss the pieces with the sugar in the small baking dish, and sprinkle water over them. Grate a little nutmeg on top. Make the topping by cutting the butter into small pieces. Rub the butter, flour, and sugar together through your fingers until crumbly. Scatter this mixture over the pear, and bake in a preheated 375° oven for 40 minutes. If the topping is not as brown as you'd like it, slip the dish under the broiler to brown lightly. Eat warm, with some heavy cream or a spoonful or so of the creamy top of yogurt.

Variations

You can, of course, make this dish with apples, and rhubarb is good, too. In both cases, particularly with rhubarb, you will need to add more sugar to the fruit.

A Baked Apple

Try to get good country apples—firm, juicy, and with a tart flavor. This version of a baked apple includes some indigenous Northeast Kingdom products.

WHAT YOU NEED

A good-sized tart apple	1½–2 tablespoons maple syrup
1 tablespoon Gooseberry Jam (page 240)	A couple of chopped walnuts, or butternuts if you can find them
A dab of butter	
A sprinkling of ground cinnamon	Heavy cream (optional)

Core the apple at the stem end, and set it in a small baking dish. Stuff the gooseberry jam into the hollow. Top with a little butter and a sprinkling of cinnamon. Pour the maple syrup on top, and sprinkle a pinch of cinnamon and the chopped walnuts over all. Bake in a preheated 350° oven for 1 hour. Enjoy it warm with chilled heavy cream, if that pleases you.

Apple Maple Bread Pudding

Every summer, I get my share of the syrup from my maple trees in northern Vermont that my cousin John taps in the spring. I particularly like the dark syrup he produces, and I devise ways to use it in old-fashioned desserts like this one. I also use the tart apples from a Duchess tree that embraces the house. So I consider this dessert a gift of nature, and I hope you'll find your own good sources for its ingredients.

WHAT YOU NEED

1 small tart apple	2 tablespoons maple syrup
1 cup slightly stale, good white bread, crusts removed, cut into small pieces	2 teaspoons sugar
	⅛ teaspoon ground cinnamon
1½ tablespoons melted butter	Garnish: heavy cream

Peel and core the apple, and cut it into chunks. Heat a couple of tablespoons of water in a small heavy pot, and toss in the apple. Lower the heat, cover, and cook, stirring a few times, for about 5 minutes, or until the apple is soft; if it isn't, cook a little longer, adding a splash more water if needed. Mix the bread pieces with the butter and maple syrup, then stir in the cooked apple. Transfer the pudding ingredients to a baking dish—a Pyrex one about 4 inches in diameter would be fine, as would a one-serving shallow baking dish. Mix the sugar and cinnamon together, and sprinkle on top. Bake in a preheated 375° oven for 20–25 minutes, or until bubbly and brown on top. Eat with heavy cream, if you like.

Summer Pudding

I always remember my childhood summers in Vermont as a procession of summer puddings made with raspberries, blueberries, blackberries, or currants as they came along. This old-fashioned dessert couldn't be simpler to put together, and you can do a single portion in a small cup mold. You can even make Summer Pudding in winter when you may have bought from the local street stand more berries imported from South America than you can eat up.

WHAT YOU NEED

¾ cup blueberries, or other berries (see headnote)

1 tablespoon or more sugar

2 very thin slices white homemade-type bread*

Garnish: heavy cream

*If you can't find really thin-sliced white bread (such as Arnold's), you can use the standard slice and cut it in half horizontally with a serrated bread knife—not an easy task, but if it breaks, you just patch the pieces back together.

Put the berries and sugar in a small saucepan with ¼ cup water. Set over low heat and let cook until soft, not more than 5 minutes. Remove from the heat. Taste when cool enough and add more sugar, if needed.

Meanwhile, remove the crusts from the bread and line a 1-cup mold with one slice of the bread, pressing it firmly into the bottom of the cup and up the sides. Tear off pieces of the second slice of bread to fill the gaps in the sides. Pour the berries and their juice into the lined mold and fold any overlapping bread on the top, then fill in the uncovered area on top with the remaining bread. Press down so the juices seep into all of the bread, put a plate on top, and refrigerate for several hours or overnight. When you're ready to eat the pudding, loosen the sides with a knife and then turn the mold upside down onto a plate. It should slip out easily. Enjoy with heavy cream, lightly whipped, if you wish.

Homemade Ice Cream

Another of the treats of summer was making ice cream, cracking up the big block of ice and taking turns with the crank—hard work that was rewarded by getting to lick the dasher when the ice cream was ready. Today we can buy convenient small ice cream makers that allow you to put the freezer bowl into the freezer so there's no chopping of ice and the churning goes much faster. I particularly like making my own ice cream because I can use pure ripe seasonal fruits and berries and pure cream, without all the additives of candies and cookies that go into the commercial varieties today. Also, it's a good way to preserve berries if I've been tempted to stop at a nearby farm where you can pick your own—and I inevitably pick more than I can eat up.

WHAT YOU NEED

1 cup mashed strawberries or peaches (peeled and pitted) or other berries and fruits

3 to 4 tablespoons sugar
½ cup heavy cream
¼ cup light cream

Put the bowl of your ice cream maker into the freezer 24 hours ahead (I usually keep it there all summer).

Mix the mashed berries or other fruit with 3 tablespoons of the sugar, then taste critically and add more if you like. Stir in the creams and pour everything into the icy bowl of the ice cream maker. Follow the manufacturer's directions for freezing.

Panna Cotta with Maple Syrup

I saw this on the menu at an Italian restaurant, and although I did not order it, I liked the idea of using a little of my own dark maple syrup to lend its flavor to the delicate, creamy custard. So I developed this recipe through trial and error. That's another advantage of cooking something just for yourself: you're the guinea pig, and you can work out all the nuances before you make the dish for company. This recipe makes enough for two, so either share it or treat yourself to a second helping later in the week.

WHAT YOU NEED

¼ cup confectioners' sugar

2 tablespoons maple syrup, plus a little more for optional garnish

½ cup milk

1 cup heavy cream

¾ teaspoon unflavored gelatin

Garnish: blueberries, blackberries, raspberries, strawberries, or a combination (optional)

Mix the sugar, maple syrup, milk, and cream together in a small saucepan, and heat, stirring. As soon as bubbles appear around the edges, remove the pan from the heat. Sprinkle in the gelatin, stirring vigorously, and continue to stir for 3–4 minutes. Let cool completely, giving an occasional stir. Now pour the cooled custard into two custard cups or glass dishes, cover with plastic wrap, and refrigerate overnight. You can unmold the panna cotta and drizzle a little bit more maple syrup around it, garnishing, if you like, with some berries. Or you can enjoy the panna cotta straight from the cup.

Feeding Unexpected Guests

If you have followed my advice about stocking your freezer and fridge and cupboard with useful items, you won't be at a loss when family or friends show up and you urge them to stay and have something to eat. Here are some suggestions for dishes that you can easily make:

- A good substantial soup. Draw on your freezer for stock, look in the vegetable bin for some aromatic vegetables, add a little rice or pasta or grains to give it body, and in less than half an hour you'll have a hearty soup ready. You can also add some slices of sausage or ham, float some croutons on top, and grate cheese over all.
- A frittata made in a big ovenproof skillet (count on two eggs per person). First sauté in butter or olive oil some sliced onions, potatoes, red or green peppers, and any other colorful, firm vegetable, such as asparagus, zucchini, or fennel. When they have softened, add the eggs and any cooked meat you want to include, and cook very slowly, covered, until the eggs are set. Grate a generous amount of cheese over the top, and slip the skillet under the broiler so that the cheese melts. For guidance, see page 104 and just multiply the amounts according to how many hungry eaters you have.
- Individual omelets. This is doable for six people. Just get the fillings warm and ready; see page 103 for ideas, and follow the technique described there. I find cracking the eggs into a quart-size measuring cup with spout, if you have one, is helpful. Then pour ½ cup of the beaten eggs into the omelet pan to make one omelet. Otherwise, a bowl is fine, and you can scoop up the right amount with a ½-cup measure. Have someone ready with warm plates to take each omelet to the table as you make the next.
- A pasta dish. See pages 181–187 for lots of suggestions.
- A tian or shallow casserole of cooked rice and vegetables with grated cheese on top. See page 173.

- A strata made with layers of vegetables, ham or leftover meat, cheese, and bread and baked. See page 113.
- A substantial salad. See what's in your fridge—or in the garden—and toss everything together. Chunks of yesterday's bread soaked in the dressing add substance, as would any leftover cooked chicken, fish, or meat. Look through the salad sections (pages 146–157) for ideas.
- Cheese and fruit are your best bet for dessert. If you don't have enough fruit to go around, supplement with dried figs and nuts. And it's a good idea always to have some cookies in the cookie jar.

Gooseberry Jam

I realize that not everyone has two gooseberry bushes growing right outside his or her house, but I do, and so I give myself over on a long summer afternoon to making gooseberry jam. I never have nearly enough (and I usually double the recipe below), because I use it on so many things during the winter, always reminding me poignantly of summer days, and my friends and relatives like it so much that they all get some for Christmas. So it's worth the effort of topping and tailing the berries and watching the pot anxiously as the berries boil. I always feel so good when the jam is finally all tucked away in jars.

The gooseberries should still be green when you pick them (or buy them at a farmers' market). If they've turned pink, they are too ripe and have lost a lot of their tart flavor. The jam turns mysteriously dark rose red as it cooks, so the final confection is a handsome color.

WHAT YOU NEED

> 1 quart gooseberries
> 4 cups sugar
> ¾ cup water

Top and tail the gooseberries—meaning, remove the hard brown stem and the little dark spot on the tail. You can do this with a sharp knife, or just use your thumbnail. Wash the berries, and put them in a large pot with the sugar and water. Bring to a boil, turn the heat down a bit, and boil steadily, stirring often, for about 15 minutes.

Start testing. First, scoop up a spoonful of the boiling jam, and let it fall back into the pot. If it falls in drops that begin to hold together as one, it is done. I always double-check by putting a saucer in the fridge, or briefly in the freezer, and spooning a little of the boiling jam onto that. If the jam holds together and wrinkles slightly when you push it, that means it is done. If not, continue to cook it. You'll probably have to make several tests before you get it right, and sometimes it takes much longer than you think it will.

Meanwhile, pour boiling water into either four 1-cup jelly jars or two pint jars. When the jam is done, empty the jars and pour the boiling jam into them, right up to the top, then seal them. If you find that your jam is too thin when you open the first jar, you can boil up all the jam again and give it another 4–5 minutes of cooking.

Preserved Lemons

I learned from Claudia Roden, who brought the secrets of Middle Eastern cooking to this country in the 1960s, how to make this invaluable preserve, which adds zest to so many dishes. I even find that you can use a little of it in place of fresh lemons to perk up a dish.

WHAT YOU NEED

8 or 9 lemons

4 tablespoons salt (I use kosher)

Quarter four of the lemons lengthwise, not quite cutting through the bottoms. Spread each one open, and rub a tablespoon of salt all over it. Pack the four salted lemons snugly into a jar, screw the cover on tightly, and store in a cool place or refrigerate. After three days, squeeze at least four of the remaining lemons, and pour their juice into the jar. The liquid should just cover the salted lemons; if not, add the juice of another lemon. Do not use for a month. These preserved lemons will keep indefinitely in the refrigerator.

To use, cut off the portion of lemon you need, and scrape away and discard the pulp. Rinse the rind to remove salt.

Roasted Red Peppers

I use red peppers a lot, but they are grown so large these days that more often than not, I find myself with a quarter or a half that needs to be used up. The solution is to roast them and store them in olive oil. In fact, I've become so fond of my roasted peppers that I'll sometimes make up a batch on the weekend to see me through the days ahead.

If you have gas burners, use this top-of-the-stove method rather than doing them in the oven (if you don't have gas burners, see page 143 for roasting). Because they become thoroughly charred all over, they develop a wonderful smoky flavor.

WHAT YOU NEED

1 large red bell pepper and/or any good-sized leftover pieces

Olive oil

Put a grill rack, if you have one, over the gas burner of your stove. Cut the pepper lengthwise into four or six pieces, depending on size, and scrape out the pith and seeds. Rub both sides with a little olive oil. Trim the ends, where the pepper curls over, so that each piece will lie flat. Turn on the burner to medium high, and lay the pieces, skin side down, flat on the grill. If you haven't got a grill, you can usually balance your pieces on the spokes of the burner or hold them on prongs of a large serving fork, right in or over the flame. Let cook for about 4 minutes, until charred on the bottom, then turn the pieces with your tongs, and grill the other side. Every now and then, flatten the pieces with a spatula and try to expose all spots to the heat. Eight to 10 minutes of grilling should suffice. Remove the peppers, and quickly pop them into a paper bag. Twist the top firmly, to keep the steam in, and let rest for at least 5 minutes. Now scrape all the charred skin off, and cut the peppers into strips. Put them in a small jar and cover them with olive oil. Screw on the top, and keep refrigerated.

Soft-Shell Crabs

Soft-shell crabs are one of the great luxuries of spring. They may be expensive if you're feeding them to a crowd. But just for one person, why not treat yourself? If the soft-shell crabs are good-sized, I'll eat only two, but I prefer the small ones and can devour three easily along with a spring vegetable. I usually buy them from a fishmonger at the end of the day. That way, he can do the killing and the cleaning, because they will be popped into the pan as soon as I get home.

WHAT YOU NEED

2 or 3 soft-shell crabs
About ⅓ cup milk
½ cup flour
⅓ cup panko and ⅓ cup
   breadcrumbs, or all
   breadcrumbs
Salt and freshly ground pepper

A pinch of ancho chili powder
   (optional)
2 tablespoons light olive oil
½ lemon
1 tablespoon or more butter
A small handful of chopped fresh
   parsley

Dip the soft-shell crabs in the milk. Toss together on a piece of wax paper the flour and the panko and breadcrumbs, and season with salt, pepper, and ancho chili powder, if using. Heat the oil in a heavy skillet that will accommodate the crabs. When it's sizzling, shake off the excess milk and dip the crabs in the crumb mixture. Slip them into the pan, and sauté on one side for 2–3 minutes, until crusty and golden brown, then turn and brown the other side—about 5 minutes in all. Remove the crabs to a warm plate, and squeeze lemon juice over them. Quickly wipe out the hot pan, and over medium heat swirl at least a tablespoon of butter—more, if you like—around in it, until the butter turns brown. Pour the browned butter over the crabs, and sprinkle parsley on top. Eat immediately.

Second round? None on this. I always lick the plate clean.

Experimenting with a Japanese Fish

When you are cooking for yourself, above all have fun. If you feel like experimenting with something new, do it. If what you turn out is disappointing, only you will be disappointed—and in the process you have probably learned something from it. If it's ambrosia, you can wallow fully in this new delight, savoring each bite with no distractions. And you have something new to serve guests.

Recently I had a soba-soup lunch with Hiroko Shimbo, author of *The Sushi Experience,* and afterward we shopped at the Sunset Market upstairs on Stuyvesant Street, in the East Village neighborhood of Manhattan, to replenish my dwindling supply of Japanese products. As well as taking home a package of their *unagi kabawaki,* that delicious broiled eel that is a delight to have on hand for improvising Japanese-style, I wanted an unusual fish for dinner that night, and I asked Hiroko what she would recommend. She immediately picked out a vacuum-sealed package of *hamachi kama.* It was an odd-looking piece of fish—just a rim of flesh sticking to the collarbone, with a fin poking out one side—but I fully trusted Hiroko's instincts. I looked forward all afternoon to the experiment, and I couldn't have been more delightfully rewarded.

The piece of fish was about ½ pound, and Hiroko told me to rub salt on both sides of it and leave it for 20 minutes before washing the salt off. Then I put the fish less than 2 inches below a hot broiler and broiled it for 4 minutes on each side. That's it. All the *hamachi kama* needed was a squirt of lemon. The flesh was deliciously succulent, once again proof that close to the bone is best, and it was fun to pick up the collarbone and suck the meat out of the crevices—one of the perks of eating alone. With it I had a silky Purée of Celery Root and Potatoes (page 134), which seemed just right.

Sautéed Scallops

As a child, and well into adulthood, I was allergic to scallops. But little by little I got over it. It can happen; the body does change. So I've been making up for my years of deprivation and quite often treat myself to a full plate of carefully cooked sea scallops.

I remember Julia Child emphasizing how important it was to use a large pan, so the scallops would have plenty of space to brown. And because they needed to cook over high heat, clarified butter was essential. We were once having lunch at an elegant French restaurant in New York, which will be nameless, and Julia ordered scallops. After her first bite, she put down her fork and proclaimed that the chef hadn't used clarified butter. As she tucked away most of the flawed dish, she emphasized again the importance of using clarified butter when browning over high heat, although she did admit that most Americans aren't going to take the trouble to clarify their own butter, and that it was okay for the home cook to use half butter and half light vegetable oil, which would temper the burning. I am always careful to watch the pan, as if Julia is still looking over my shoulder, whenever I make this dish.

WHAT YOU NEED

⅓ pound very fresh sea scallops*
All-purpose flour for dredging
2 teaspoons butter
2 teaspoons light olive oil
Salt and freshly ground pepper

1 fat shallot, minced
A splash of white wine
A sprinkling of chopped fresh
  parsley

*One way to judge freshness is to make sure the scallops aren't sitting in a pool of liquid. Also, smell them if you can.

Dredge the scallops in flour. Heat the butter and oil in a large heavy skillet over high heat, and when it is sizzling, shake the excess flour from the scallops and scatter them in the hot pan. Keep the heat high, and turn and move the scallops around frequently, giving the pan a shake now and then. Total cooking time should not be more than 3 minutes—or 4 for really large pieces. Season the scallops lightly with salt and several grindings of the pepper mill, and remove them to a warm plate. Lower the heat to moderate, and toss the shallot into the pan. Stir it around for about 30 seconds, splash in the wine, and let it reduce slightly. Pour this sauce over the scallops, scraping up every bit of pan juice with a spatula. Sprinkle the parsley on top.

Variation

Sometimes I wrap a band of prosciutto around the circumference of each scallop and secure it with a toothpick. These can be broiled, or sautéed as above. The sharp saltiness of the prosciutto, along with the briny taste of the scallops, creates a striking combination of flavors.

Shad Roe with Sorrel Sauce

I had never cooked with sorrel until I worked with André Soltner on his Lutèce cookbook. He was then the devoted chef-owner of the restaurant, on East Fiftieth Street in Manhattan, but he never forgot his roots in Alsace. There, leafy green sorrel is common, and its tart flavor accents any number of dishes. So it was not surprising that when André was developing a sauce for that quintessential American specialty, shad roe, his secret ingredient was sorrel. However, sorrel was not so easy to find in markets in those days, and André would have to bring an armful of handpicked sorrel from his own garden in the Catskills down to the Lutèce kitchen, so as not to disappoint his loyal customers.

Later, when my husband and I bought our summer place in the Northeast Kingdom of Vermont, we discovered that wild sorrel grew abundantly in the surrounding woods and in the garden. I even planted a cultivated variety to make sure we had enough, and I soon dubbed sorrel, along with gooseberries, the lemons of the North.

And now that Lutèce is no more, and I can't enjoy a lunch there, I celebrate this spring delight by making myself André's delectable shad roe with sorrel sauce.

WHAT YOU NEED

FOR THE SAUCE	FOR THE SHAD ROE
2 teaspoons butter	2 teaspoons butter
1 generous cup sorrel leaves	1 pair shad roe
Salt and freshly ground pepper	A splash of milk
Pinch of sugar	Flour
¼ cup heavy cream	Salt and freshly ground pepper

Melt the butter for the sauce in a small pan. Drop in the sorrel leaves, and cook over medium heat, stirring now and then, until the liquid has evaporated. The sorrel will turn a khaki color, but don't let that bother you. Season with salt and pepper and just a tiny pinch of sugar. Pour in the cream, and cook for about 5 minutes, until thickened. Keep warm.

Heat the remaining 2 teaspoons butter in a small skillet that will just hold the shad roe. Rub the milk over the roe, dredge in flour, season with salt and pepper, and slip the roe into the pan. Cook slowly for about 5 minutes, turning once. Arrange on a warm plate, and spoon the sauce around.

Sea Urchins

Although sea urchins are abundant in our North Atlantic waters, Americans have never really taken to them the way the French have embraced them. There, *oursins,* as they are called, are often included on raw-seafood platters and appear in many guises in the creations of haute-cuisine chefs. So I was delighted when I spotted these spiny-shelled mollusks about the size of a woman's compact, though plumper, sitting on ice at Citarella's excellent fish counter, and I immediately snapped up an expensive dozen. The truth is that they are really at their best eaten raw, just scooped out of the shell. So that's what I planned to do as soon as I got them home.

To open the sea urchin, I used the point of a sharp knife to pierce the slightly soft orifice in the center of one side. Then I switched to scissors and cut all around, about ½ inch out from that orifice, to make a round lid that I could pull out. I carefully drained off the seawater and blackish brine, and there exposed was the pinkish-tan coral nestled in the bottom shell. As I reached for a small grapefruit spoon, and was about to plunge in, I saw the creature twitch and start to wriggle. I was unnerved. But then I felt ashamed. I eat live oysters and clams, and drop wriggling lobsters into boiling water, after all. And I did want to taste those *oursins.* So my appetite prevailed, and I sat down to a plateful of them, and relished every delectable mouthful.

For those of you who may be more squeamish, Lidia Bastianich uses sea urchins in a simple, unadorned recipe for pasta. You must never heat them up; they are simply folded into the thin pasta strands just out of the pot, and the combination is perfection.

So experiment, and try new things. You have only yourself to please.

Osso Buco with Gremolata

I'm sure every cook who loves Italian food has a special recipe for osso buco. But I'm not so sure that anyone has a recipe to serve one, because it's not the sort of thing you make for just one person. But it's simple to reduce. The crucial factor is the pot; you need that heavy 4-cup pot with its own lid, so that your shank piece just fits into it and the liquid level stays almost to the top of the meat while it is simmering. That way, you don't require too much cooking liquid, and the flavor develops intensity. I sometimes make this on a Saturday afternoon, when an Italian opera is playing on the radio, and just hearing the singing and smelling the osso buco as it perks away on the stove heightens my anticipation of a lovely meal to come.

WHAT YOU NEED

2 teaspoons olive oil

Salt

One 2-inch veal shank, cut across
    the bone

1 small-to-medium onion,
    chopped

½ carrot, peeled and chopped

1 medium tomato, chopped

1 small leek, or ½ large leek,
    cut into ½-inch pieces

¼ cup white wine

½ cup chicken broth

Freshly ground pepper

Small sprig of fresh rosemary,
    or a pinch of dried

5 or 6 fresh parsley stems

GREMOLATA

1 small garlic clove, peeled and
    minced

About 2 strips lemon peel
    (without pith), minced (about
    1 teaspoon)

1 tablespoon chopped fresh
    parsley

Heat the oil in your small pot. Rub salt over the veal shank, and put it into the sizzling oil. Brown lightly on one side, then turn and brown the other. Turn the veal on its side to make room for the onion, carrot, tomato, and leek pieces. Sauté them for a minute or two, then flip the shank over so it is bone side down, and pour in the wine. Stir to get up any browned bits, and reduce the wine by half. Pour in the broth; add several grindings of pepper, lay the rosemary and parsley stems on top, and cover. Let cook for 1¾ hours at a gentle simmer.

Meanwhile, put together the gremolata—the tasty, garlicky topping—by simply mixing the minced garlic, lemon peel, and parsley together.

When the meat is very tender, remove it to a warm plate, discarding the parsley stems, and sprinkle the top with as much of the gremolata as you like. Eat with some crusty bread to sop up the sauce. And don't forget the marrow. Use a little coffee spoon to scrape it out and extract the last precious morsel.

A Small Cassoulet

It may seem crazy even to think of making a cassoulet for oneself, although this one may be large enough to share with a friend. But if you have all the different elements, it's not much more than an assembly job. You just have to think ahead. So, when you have that Small Roast Pork Tenderloin (page 42), set aside three or four little chunks of the flavorful cooked meat (they can be frozen and labeled "for future cassoulet"). Then plan on having Braised Shoulder Lamb Chops (page 48), which is always more than I can eat in one sitting, and use that extra braised chop (it can also be frozen), along with a lot of the good juices, to be the mainstay of your cassoulet. One can usually get a good pork sausage these days; even if you have to mail-order it, it's a staple item worth keeping in the freezer. So there you are: start your beans the night before, and put this heavenly bean dish together on a wintry day off, letting it fill your kitchen with its tantalizing aromas. You won't regret it.

When I suggested to Julia Child that she include a recipe for this great dish in Mastering the Art of French Cooking, *there really weren't any good fresh garlic sausages available to buy, so Julia agreed that she had better work out a formula for making them at home. Several days later, I went up to Cambridge, Massachusetts, where the Childs lived, to work on the book with her, and I found that one wall of the kitchen was covered in notes on the work she had done to develop a formula for the authentic garlic sausage for cassoulet. Her research had taken her back to early French charcuterie books, and she'd made notes on each of her testings, ending up with her own carefully worked-out recipe. I gasped at her meticulous research, and then asked tentatively if maybe this might not be beyond the reach of the American home cook, but she reassured me. "No, not at all," she said. "It's really as easy as making hamburgers."*

WHAT YOU NEED

⅓ cup Great Northern beans

2 teaspoons duck fat, if you have it, or vegetable oil

1 small onion, chopped

½ carrot, chopped

½ rib celery, chopped

1 garlic clove, peeled and slivered

A splash of red wine

Several sprigs parsley with stems

Pinch of dried thyme

⅓ bay leaf

¾ cup duck, goose, or chicken stock, or more if needed

Salt and freshly ground pepper

3 or 4 chunks pork left over from A Small Roast Pork Tenderloin (page 42)

3 or 4 pieces Braised Shoulder Lamb Chops (page 48) with aromatic vegetables

¼ pound garlic sausage, sliced fairly thick and lightly browned

¼ cup breadcrumbs mixed with a little chopped fresh parsley

Duck or goose fat or butter for dotting the top

"Quick soak" the beans: Put them in a small cooking pot and cover with 2 cups water. Bring to a boil, let boil heartily for 2 minutes, then turn off the heat, cover, and let sit for 1 hour.

Close to the end of the hour during which your beans have been soaking, heat the fat in another fairly small, heavy cooking pot, and sauté the onion, carrot, celery, and garlic until the vegetables are limp—about 3 minutes. Splash in the wine, and let it cook down briefly. Now transfer the beans and their cooking water to this pot, and add the parsley, thyme, and bay leaf. Add enough stock to bring the liquid level up to about 1 inch above the beans, bring to a boil, then simmer for about 1 hour or more, with cover askew, until the beans are just tender. Salt them now, and add several grindings of pepper. Fish out the parsley and bay leaf, and spoon a layer of beans into a small casserole, cover with the pork and lamb, another layer of beans, a layer of sausage slices, and a final layer of beans. Pour the bean cooking liquid into the casserole, and add enough stock to come halfway up. Sprinkle the parsleyed breadcrumbs on top, and dot the surface with small amounts of fat. Bake in a preheated 350° oven for 1 hour.

Braised Sweetbreads Marsala with Honey Mushrooms

I adore sweetbreads, but, alas, they are becoming increasingly hard to get. So, whenever I see a package of them in the supermarket, I snatch them up and give myself a treat. I'm apt to vary the aromatics, but basically the technique is the same. If you do all the preparation in the morning, or even the night before, the final sautéing with just the right complementary flavors takes about 15 minutes. And when you have your first bite, there is something so deeply satisfying about the tender creamy texture of sweetbreads, and their ability to absorb and transform the aromatic flavors you give them, that you feel a small miracle has taken place. No wonder they are called sweetbreads.

WHAT YOU NEED

About ⅓ pound calves' sweetbreads

½ lemon

Salt

About 2 tablespoons loosely packed dried honey mushrooms

1 tablespoon butter

1 shallot, chopped

All-purpose flour for dredging

Marsala wine

2 teaspoons *glace de viande,* or about 3 tablespoons beef stock

Freshly ground pepper

The night before or the morning of the day you plan to cook your sweetbreads, or at least several hours before, put them in a small pot with enough water to cover by 2 inches. Squeeze the juice of the half-lemon into the pot, and add a good pinch of salt. Bring to a boil, and then reduce the heat to a lively simmer and cook for 15 minutes. Drain the sweetbreads, and plunge them into cold water. When they are cool enough to handle, carefully open up the lobes just enough to ease out some of the connective tissue. You won't get it all, but don't worry. Now put the sweetbreads on a small plate, put another plate on top, and set something heavy on it—a jar of jam or a soup can. Refrigerate for an hour or so, or overnight.

About 20 minutes before cooking, soak the dried honey mushrooms in ¾ cup warm water.

When ready to cook, melt the butter in a small skillet and sauté the shallot until softened. Break the sweetbreads up into about six pieces, following the lobes, and dredge the pieces in lightly salted flour. Toss them into the pan, and sauté for 4–5 minutes, until lightly browned. Pour in a good splash of Marsala, and let it cook down until almost evaporated. Strain the soaked honey mushrooms, reserving the straining water, and toss them into the pan. Sauté together for another minute before adding the mushroom soaking liquid and the *glace de viande* or stock. Turn the heat down, cover, and let braise for about 10 minutes, checking frequently to see that there is enough sauce, and adding a little water and/or stock as necessary. Taste, correct seasonings, and add some freshly ground pepper.

Enjoy this delight with some steamed new potatoes and/or fresh peas or other compatible seasonal vegetable.

Variations

Of course, different kinds of mushrooms can be substituted, including fresh, but I find that using at least some dried mushrooms gives an intensity to the sauce. And Madeira is every bit as good as Marsala here.

Steamed Lobster

I decided to make lobster the last recipe in this book so I could give myself the gift of a lobster dinner to celebrate. My father's family in Montpelier, Vermont, were all passionate lobster-lovers. Being in an inland state, cut off from the sea, only made them more avid for a good lobster dinner, and they frequented The Lobster Pot on Main Street for every kind of celebration. My aunt Marian, after she became a widow, would often stroll down to The Lobster Pot to have dinner by herself, and it was there that she taught me the ritual of eating a lobster—sucking the juices and little morsels of flesh from each leg, and always saving the big claws for the last, because to her they contained the most delicious meat.

So, for my treat, I stopped at Citarella's in Manhattan and asked for a 1¼-pounder. The fishmonger held one up to demonstrate for me how lively the little lobster was as it wriggled and pawed the air with its tentacles. I was even asked whether I wanted a male or a female, and of course I said female, so I could enjoy the roe. But when I got it home, there was only the tomalley— the green-gray loose substance that is the liver; there was no roe. I looked in Julia Child's The Way to Cook and realized that I should have checked first for the little swimmerets under the tail: the male's are "clean and pointed," whereas the female's are "fringed with hair"—a test that is not easy to execute when the creature is wriggling desperately.

I have always preferred steaming to boiling, because that way the lobster doesn't get too immersed in water, and the small amount of steaming water becomes more intense. So I hauled down my largest pot, and arranged a collapsible steamer inside it.

WHAT YOU NEED

1 ¼-pound live lobster
2 tablespoons butter
½ lemon

Set up a collapsible steamer in a very large pot. Pour in a good inch of water and bring to a boil. Lower the lobster into the pot, on top of the steamer; slap on the lid and hold it there for the first minute or so of cooking, to keep the lobster firmly in place. Meanwhile, melt the butter slowly in a small pot, and squeeze in as much lemon juice as you like. Keep warm.

After 10 minutes of cooking, remove the lobster with tongs, and let the water drip back into the pot. Place on a big plate, with the melted butter in a small cup alongside. If you don't have lobster-eating equipment, look in your toolbox for something to crack the tough shells, or use a nutcracker. I use poultry shears to cut through the middle from head to tail, so I can break the body open and get at the meat. Dip each bite into the melted butter, and relish the delectable sweet, sea-scented flavor. And be sure to spoon out the tomalley, now greenish in color and creamy in texture, and glorious to eat.

Second Round

Return the shells to the broth, and cook together for about 15 minutes, adding a little more water. You'll now have a fine broth to use in any fish soup, or for the base of a New England Bouillabaisse (page 91).

Acknowledgments

First, I want to thank all the talented cooks I have been privileged to work with over the years. They opened up new worlds to me and gave me the tools to think for myself as a cook, to experiment, and, above all, to enjoy.

As to the house of Knopf where I have worked now for some fifty-two years, I am indebted to so many of my colleagues and mentors that it is impossible to express my appreciation to all. So I'll limit myself here to thanking Sonny Mehta, who believed in the project, and those who were directly connected with the making of this book: my editor, Jonathan Segal, who encouraged me, asked sharp questions, kept me focused, and shared my love of good home cooking (particularly French); Jon's assistant, Joey McGarvey, another cooking enthusiast; Ken Schneider, my assistant of many years, who is always there for me; Carol Carson, who created the enticing jacket, and Kristen Bearse, who fashioned a lovely design for the book based on the pattern of the dish towel on the cover; Maria Massey, who shepherded the book through production; and Terry Zaroff-Evans, who copyedited with her usual sensitivity. And what would I do without Kathy Hourigan, who not only kept the ball rolling but whose enthusiasm spurred me on.

I have always loved working with Christopher Hirsheimer, whose photographs manage to capture the distinctive personality of every book she illustrates, and I am particularly grateful for her partnership in this book.

Finally, a special thanks to my stepdaughter, Bronwyn Dunne, who photographed the boxful of chanterelles (page 128) and to my son, Chris Vandercook, who caught with his camera some Vermont moments: the bounty of the garden (page 123), me at the stove (page 73) and at the chopping board (page 205), and one of my small pizzas, ready for the oven (page 212).

Index

Page references in *italic* refer to illustrations.

spinach, in egg dishes, 99, 103, 114, 228
squash (summer):
  roasting, 144
  see also zucchini
squash (winter):
  roasting, 144
  Soup, 88
stir-fried:
  Pork with Vegetables, 44–5
  Vegetables, 145
stocks:
  Beef, 82
  Chicken, 81
  homemade, substitutes for, 83
  storing in ice trays, 82
  turkey, making from carcass, 22
  see also broths
Strata: A Savory Custard, 113–14, 239
  Turkey, Vegetable, and Cheese, 23
stuffed:
  Eggplant, 125–6
  Green Peppers or Zucchini, 126
  Portobello, 126–7
  Potato, Baked, 127
substitutions, 5
sugar, vanilla, 224
Summer Pudding, 234, *235*
Sushi Experience, The (Shimbo), 176, 244
Sushi Rice Vegetable Salad, 176–7
Sweetbreads, Braised, Marsala with Honey Mushrooms, 252–4

Tabbouleh, 155–6
tarts, individual:
  Apple, 229–30
  Quiche for One, 227–8, *228*
  Rhubarb, Pear, or Berry, 230
Tenth Muse, The (Jones), vii, 29, 53
Tettrazini, Turkey, 23
tians, 238

of Rice and Greens, Provençal, 173–4
  Zucchini, 174
tilapia, in Fillet of Fish in Parchment, 64–8, *65, 66*
toast:
  Minced Chicken on, *18,* 18–19
  Welsh Rabbit, 119
tomato(es):
  Cherry, Fusilli with Mushrooms, Liver and, 182–3
  Plum, Penne with Tuna, Black Olives and, 181–2
  Ratatouille, 132–3
  roasting, 144
  Sauce, 162
Tongue, Fresh Veal, 56–7
tuna:
  and Farro Salad, 191
  Penne with Plum Tomatoes, Black Olives and, 181–2
turkey:
  leftover, uses for, 19, 22–3, 94, 103, 179, 195
  Salad, Asian-Accented, 148
  stock, making from carcass, 22
  Wings, Beans and, 202–3
turnips, roasting, 144

utensils, *8, 9*

vanilla sugar, 224
veal, 54–7
  Blanquette de Veau with Leeks, 54–5
  leftover, uses for, 55, 171–2, 195
  Osso Buco with Gremolata, 249–50
  Quick Risotto with Chestnuts, Mushrooms and, 171–2
  Sauce, Creamy, Pasta with, 55
  Tongue, Fresh, 56–7

A Note About the Author

Judith Jones is senior editor and vice president at Alfred A. Knopf. She joined the company in 1957 as an editor, working primarily on translations of the books of French writers such as Albert Camus and Jean-Paul Sartre. She had worked before that for Doubleday, first in New York and then in Paris. In addition to her literary authors, she has been particularly interested in developing a list of first-rate cookbook writers; her authors have included Julia Child (Judith published Julia's first book and was her editor ever after), Lidia Bastianich, James Beard, Marion Cunningham, Rosie Daley, Marcella Hazan, Madhur Jaffrey, Edna Lewis, Joan Nathan, Scott Peacock, Jacques Pépin, Claudia Roden, Hiroko Shimbo, and Nina Simonds. Judith is the co-author with Evan Jones (her late husband) of three books: *The Book of Bread; Knead It, Punch It, Bake It!* (for children); and *The Book of New New England Cookery*. She also collaborated with Angus Cameron on *The L. L. Bean Game and Fish Cookbook*. Recently she has contributed to *Vogue, Saveur, Bon Appétit, Gourmet,* and *Departures* magazines. She is the author of *The Tenth Muse: My Life in Food* (published in 2007). Judith Jones has been awarded lifetime achievement awards by *Bon Appétit* (2003), the James Beard Foundation (2006), and the I.A.C.P. (2007). She lives in New York City and Vermont.

A Note on the Type

This book was set in a typeface named Bulmer. This distinguished letter is a replica of a type long famous in the history of English printing that was designed and cut by William Martin about 1790 for William Bulmer of the Shakespeare Press. In design, it is all but a modern face, with vertical stress, sharp differentiation between the thick and thin strokes, and nearly flat serifs. The decorative italic shows the influence of Baskerville, as Martin was a pupil of John Baskerville's.

Composed by North Market Street Graphics,
Lancaster, Pennsylvania

Printed and bound by RR Donnelley, Inc.
Crawfordsville, Indiana

Designed by M. Kristen Bearse